SAVING OUR CHILDREN IN A WORLD GONE CRAZY

WHY WE MUST GIVE OUR CHILDREN A BIBLICAL WORLDVIEW

JEFF KEATON

RenewaNation

Published by:
RenewaNation
P.O. Box 12366
Roanoke, VA 24025
renewanation.org

Contact us to order:
info@renewanation.org

DEDICATION

We dedicate this book to our daughters, Julianna and Heidi, and their husbands, Andrew and Jordan, and to the beautiful grandchildren they have given us. In spite of our imperfect parenting, we are deeply grateful to God that our daughters and sons-in-law love Jesus and are raising our grandchildren to know, love, and serve Jesus.

Love, Dad and Mom

TABLE OF CONTENTS

SECTION 1

Biblical Worldview
Discipleship In a
World Gone Crazy

CHAPTER 1

God's Good Design

"The soul's deepest thirst is for God Himself, who has made us so that we can never be satisfied without Him."

F.F. Bruce

Over the last three decades, I have been fighting for the souls of our children through the two church ministries I led and now through the ministry of RenewaNation. I knew things were not going well thirty years ago as I walked through the halls of public schools in Broward County, Florida, but I couldn't imagine what our children would face today. The attacks against them come from every angle—education, media, entertainment, technology, and peer pressure. As Christian parents who want to see our children grow up to love Christ and all His ways, it can be absolutely overwhelming.

I wrote this book for Christian parents who have a deep desire to raise godly children, but maybe you're not exactly sure what that involves or requires of you, or perhaps you're not highly confident you're on the right track. Over and over again, parents and grandparents have approached me with tears in their eyes and told me their stories of children and grandchildren who have completely abandoned the Christian faith. I am writing this book so that you never have to experience the grief of losing a child to Satan's lies.

In this book, you will be challenged to think at a very deep level about who you are allowing to have influence in your child's life. I urge you not to get discouraged and put down the book before you have read every word. The message in this book will help you make decisions that could save your child's life and their eternal souls.

To say we live in a world gone crazy is an understatement. The things children are getting caught up in are so absurd that if we were to have written a book thirty years ago predicting where we are today, no one would have believed us.

I'll never forget the phone call I received from a hysterical mother whose seventeen-year-old son had just walked into their Christian home and announced he was going to become a woman. They hadn't seen any signs of this happening. He made this decision seemingly out of nowhere. As they resisted his desire, he told the school and hospital that he was going to kill himself because his parents' Christian beliefs would not allow them to endorse his decision. After his father endured hours of threatening discussion with a hospital employee, the state took this young man away from his parents and placed him in the home of two lesbians who allowed him to live however he desired. That's pure insanity and a parent's worst nightmare.

Lest you think this is an outlier, several states have so-called "gender-affirming care," and the state of California just passed a law that gives the state the authority to take children away from parents who do not allow them to transition.[1]

Our children are addicted to screens, porn, and video games in record numbers, and they are anxious, depressed, and suicidal like never before. In the fog of the battle, it can be very difficult to understand where the attacks are coming from and how to combat them. We often get lost in the smoke and don't know what to do. I want to begin by helping you understand from a worldview perspective what we are up against and why you must see the big picture in order to win this fight for the souls of your children.

CLASH OF BELIEF SYSTEMS

At the root of the struggle for the souls of our children is an underlying clash of belief systems or what we call *worldviews*. A worldview is simply the core set of beliefs a person has accepted as true that guides his or her thoughts and actions in life. Several times each year, I have the privilege of speaking at conferences where George Barna is also a speaker. In one of his speeches, Barna states that after forty years of researching young people, he has now concluded that the worldview or core set of beliefs a child has developed by the age of thirteen is statistically the worldview they will die with.[2] Each time I hear Barna make this statement, I am reminded of the importance of investing in the worldview development of our children from the earliest days of their lives.

Senior saints often approach me and ask, "How in the world could these kids believe what they believe today?" I tell them it's pretty simple. They were taught certain presuppositions that led them to carry out unthinkable actions in their daily lives. What may seem crazy to Judeo-Christian thinkers seems perfectly normal to them.

For example, on September 11, 2001, nineteen young men flew airplanes into buildings and killed thousands of Americans. We'd like to believe these young men had a mental illness or some other reason to do something so evil that would exclude them from guilt. However, as I have studied their actions over the years, I have concluded they did exactly what they wanted to do for one simple reason. Their minds were molded into believing a completely false worldview from the time they were small children. Adults instilled in these children the belief that if they killed infidels, God would be pleased with them and reward them greatly. They lived out their worldview to the fullest degree possible.

Every child represented by those of you reading this book is in the process of developing his or her worldview (core set of beliefs). The question is not, *"Will my child develop a worldview?"* The question is simply, *"Which worldview will my child develop?"* Foundational beliefs are being developed right now that will determine the decisions your children will make and how they will live. If we fail to teach our children the truth, the devil will make sure someone is there to tell them his lies, and they will end up living destructive lives and falling short of the meaningful life God has intended for them.

All worldviews are simply attempts to answer the greatest questions of life. Questions like: Who has ultimate authority in this world? Where did we come from? What is our purpose in life? Who makes the rules, and what rules should all humans live by? What does it mean to be human? What makes up a family? Why is there so much evil? Is there any way to fix what is broken in this world? Life's questions go on and on.

We define a worldview by how it answers these questions. Again, all worldviews, including atheism, have some kind of answer to the major questions of life. The devil and the people he controls in this world are determined to shape your children's worldview or belief system in a way that will forever lead them away from God and His truth. This is a life-and-death battle that we must not take lightly.

A biblical worldview understands reality within the context of God's good design, as discovered in God's Word, the Holy Bible. An unbiblical worldview rejects God's truth, and a hybrid worldview adopts some of God's truth along with unbiblical ideas. Many of us have a hybrid worldview, meaning we implement God's truth into our daily lives in certain areas but embrace unbiblical ideas in other areas because of secularized influences. We experience much difficulty in the areas where we do not know or live out God's good design as laid out in the Bible.

I am passionate about giving children a biblical worldview because I have become fully convinced that the biblical worldview is the only worldview that works out well in the real world. For example, God created males and females and said they should get married, stay together for life, and produce godly offspring. This is God's good design for the family, and when followed, it works out beautifully.

Worldviews have real-world consequences. When our beliefs are false, we will make decisions based on those beliefs that cause tremendous pain and suffering. When my wife was twelve years old and her brother was only five, their father rejected God's good design by abandoning his family for a life of sensuality. Thankfully, my wife has had the love of my father and family in her life since we met as young teenagers. Her dad's decision to reject God's good design has had a much more negative impact on her brother's life, and I can honestly say that he has never gotten over this devastating experience.

In our world today, millions of children identify and approve of the transgender movement. It's hard for truth-based thinkers even to fathom the foolishness of this worldview. Yet, children who have been lied to and taught an unbiblical view of sexuality and gender are embracing and living out these utterly destructive ideas.

If we want to save our children in a world gone crazy, we must become passionate and intentional about helping them develop a biblical worldview—a belief system that is fully aligned with truth. When we teach our children to live in harmony with God's good design, they will experience peace, productivity, harmony, and a taste of the paradise lost in the fall.

In this opening chapter, we've looked at a few examples of the terrible things that happen when we try to run our lives or this world in opposition to how God designed us and the world to function. In the next couple of chapters, we will examine the stories of Daniel, Shadrach, Meshach, and Abednego as a picture of the courageous people our children can become when they are trained with a biblical worldview, even while living in a godless world.

CHAPTER 2

Faithful to God In Babylon

*"Shadrach, Meshach, and Abednego answered and said to the king,
'O Nebuchadnezzar, we have no need to answer you in this matter.
If this be so, our God whom we serve is able to deliver us from the
burning fiery furnace, and he will deliver us out of your hand, O
king. But if not, be it known to you, O king, that we will not serve
your gods or worship the golden image that you have set up.'"*

Daniel 3:16-18

Every Christian parent I talk to strongly desires to see their children succeed. No one welcomes a child into the world and says, "Well, I'm sure this kid is going to be a total failure, and I can't wait to see it!" No, every parent has high hopes and dreams for their children. Christian parents usually view success as their children growing up to know, love, and serve Jesus and becoming adults who expand God's kingdom and rule in this world. How we define the finer points of ultimate success might differ from one parent to another, and how we accomplish the goal of raising successful children might be highly debatable amongst even Christian parents. However, we all agree that we want our children to grow up and not only survive but thrive in every area of their lives.

I want to give you a picture from a true account of God's work in history that will help us lock in on the ultimate goal we should have for raising our children to be successful in the eyes of God Almighty. This account is found in the book of Daniel in the Old Testament.

Daniel Taken to Babylon

In the third year of the reign of Jehoiakim king of Judah, Nebuchadnezzar king of Babylon came to Jerusalem and besieged it. And the Lord gave Jehoiakim king of Judah into his hand, with some of the vessels of the house of God. And he brought them to the land of Shinar, to the house of his god, and placed the vessels in the treasury of his god. Then the king commanded Ashpenaz, his chief eunuch, to bring some of the people of Israel, both of the royal family and of the nobility, youths without blemish, of good appearance and skillful in all wisdom, endowed with knowledge, understanding learning, and competent to stand in the king's palace, and to teach them the literature and language of the Chaldeans. The king assigned them a daily portion of the food that the king ate, and of the wine that he drank. They were to be educated for three years, and at the end of that time they were to stand before the king. Among these were Daniel, Hananiah, Mishael, and Azariah of the tribe of Judah. And the chief of the eunuchs gave them names: Daniel he called Belteshazzar, Hananiah he called Shadrach, Mishael he called Meshach, and Azariah he called Abednego.

Daniel's Faithfulness

But Daniel resolved that he would not defile himself with the king's food, or with the wine that he drank. Therefore he asked the chief of the eunuchs to allow him not to defile himself. And God gave Daniel favor and compassion in the sight of the chief of the eunuchs, and the chief of the eunuchs said to Daniel, "I fear my lord the king, who assigned your food and your drink; for why should he see that you were in worse condition than the youths who are of your own age? So you would endanger my head with the king." Then Daniel said to the steward whom the chief of the eunuchs had assigned over Daniel, Hananiah, Mishael, and Azariah, "Test your servants for ten days; let us be given vegetables to eat and water to drink. Then let our appearance and the appearance of the youths who eat the king's food be observed by you, and deal with your servants according to what you see." So he listened to them in this matter, and tested them for ten days. At the end of ten days it was seen that they were better in appearance and fatter in flesh than all the youths who ate the king's food. So the steward took away their food and the wine they were to drink, and gave them vegetables. As for these four youths, God gave them learning and skill in all literature and wisdom, and Daniel had understanding in all visions and dreams. At the end of the time, when the king had commanded that they should be brought in, the chief of the eunuchs brought them in before Nebuchadnezzar. And the king spoke with them, and among all of them none was found like Daniel, Hananiah, Mishael, and Azariah. Therefore they stood before the king. And in every matter of wisdom and understanding about which the king inquired of them, he found them ten times better than all the magicians and enchanters that were in all his kingdom. And Daniel was there until the first year of King Cyrus (Dan. 1:1-21).

When these young men were taken captive and sent to Babylon as slaves, it was the most glamorous, successful, and powerful kingdom in the world.[1] This magnificent city was the first to surpass 200,000 in population and reached its pinnacle under King Nebuchadnezzar's leadership.[2] Babylon is mentioned 280 times in the Bible, sometimes as the actual city and, in many other instances, as a symbol of the world's system that has rejected God.[3] Rebellion against God was at the core of Babylon from day one, and its earliest act of defiance was building the Tower of Babel. It was here to this godless city that these young men were taken to serve the purposes of King Nebuchadnezzar, and yet they refused to defy God even under threat of death (Dan. 3:16-18). *What must have happened in their young lives to have them so ready for that battle at such a young age?*

As I looked with fresh eyes at this account, what caught my attention the most was that someone had prepared these young men for the moment when they would be separated from their families and homeland and face an ultimate decision about who they would serve. Even more impressive is the simple fact that they were likely only young teenagers when they had to make these life-determining decisions.

There are remarkable similarities between the ancient world these young men were taken into and the modern world our children and grandchildren are growing up in right now. There has never been a more prosperous, glamorous, powerful, pleasure-seeking culture in the history of the world than the one our children are growing up in today. This worldly system surrounding our children desires to have them, and the allurement of accepting the call of our world is overwhelmingly powerful. When I look at these Hebrew young men, I am encouraged to believe that if we train our children well, our young people can be prepared to thrive in the Babylon we live in today.

ALTERED IDENTITY

These four Hebrew slaves were recognized as some of the best and brightest of all the captives, and in his desire that these young men serve him, Nebuchadnezzar first changed their names and identities. All four young men had Hebrew names that honored the one true God of heaven. Notice the names Nebuchadnezzar gave them that honored the four main Babylonian gods: Bel, the chief god, and the gods of the sun, moon, and fire.

Daniel's name in Hebrew means *"God is my judge."*[4]

His Babylonian name was *Belteshazzar,* which means *"Bel protect his life."* Bel was the Babylonian's chief God.[5]

Hananiah's name in Hebrew means *"Yah has been gracious."*[6]

His Babylonian name was *Shadrach,* which means *"inspired or illumined by the Sun God."*[7]

Mishael's name in Hebrew means *"who is what God is."*

His Babylonian name, *Meshach*, means *"who is what Aku is."*[8] Aku is the Babylonian god of the moon.

Azariah's name in Hebrew means *"Yah has helped."*

His Babylonian name, *Abednego*, means *"servant of Nebo,"* a Babylonian god associated with Mercury.[9]

Notice that the suffix -el in Daniel's and Mishael's Hebrew names refers to *Elohim*, one of the names of the God of Israel. Azariah and Hananiah contain the suffix -iah or -yah, which is God's covenant name, *Yahweh*.[10]

To fully indoctrinate and reshape the thinking of these young men, Nebuchadnezzar knew he needed to change their identity in an attempt to erase everything they had been taught about the God who would compete with him for loyalty.

We live in a world today that is out to steal our children's God-given identity in every way imaginable. God created our children in His divine image, male and female. Because of this, humans are by far the most special species on this planet. He has stamped His ability to think, plan, design, speak, and write on our children and given them a divine purpose to rule well over His created order.

Satan knows he cannot capture our children unless he destroys their identity as children of the one true God, and the world he controls is hell-bent on stripping our children of their divine identity. They tell our children they are cosmic accidents with no divine purpose. They do everything in their power, especially in the areas of education and pop culture, to convince our children that God is not real, the Bible is full of falsehoods, and parents and churches are out of touch with reality. They have now gone so far as to convince millions of children that the biological sex God gave them may have been a mistake, and the only way they can know who they are is to follow their feelings and emotions. Only those who embrace this new gender paradigm and promote it are applauded and honored.

The discipleship and worldview development of children in the family, church, and school matter so much because these are places where our children's divine identity should always be protected, affirmed, and celebrated rather than stolen, challenged, and maligned. In the next chapter, we'll explore what it takes to prepare our children to embrace their God-given identity, fulfill God's plan for their lives, and thrive in today's Babylon.

CHAPTER 3

Preparing Our Children to Thrive In Babylon

"Education about God precedes and serves exultation in God. Learning truth precedes loving truth. Right reflection on God precedes right affection for God. Seeing the glory of Christ precedes savoring the glory of Christ."

John Piper

As we continue to examine this account in Daniel, let's examine three key aspects that prepared these young men to thrive in Babylon: exceptional and intentional training, moral and spiritual development, and God's favor and blessing.

THRIVING IN BABYLON WITH EXCEPTIONAL AND INTENTIONAL TRAINING

Notice the qualities that resulted in these young men being chosen for high-level service in Babylon (Dan. 1:4).

- Youths without blemish
- Of good appearance
- Skillful in all wisdom
- Endowed with knowledge
- Understanding learning
- Competent to stand in the king's palace
- Able to learn the literature and language of the Babylonians

Someone had done a fantastic job training these outstanding young men. Their education had been exceptional, and their families were super intentional, even though they grew up in a decaying and desperate time in their nation's history.

In our world today, the masses are being trained in schools where education has been so degraded that our children are falling further and further behind children all around the world. This is already causing our businesses, healthcare facilities, and every other area of society to crumble due to a lack of excellent workers.

Educational ideologies and methodologies used to train almost fifty million K-12 children in America today are no longer based on absolute truth.[1] Thus, our children are being indoctrinated with social-emotional learning (SEL) and critical theory (CRT/cultural Marxism) in its many forms involving race, sexuality, educational equity, economics, and more.

I cannot find the terms to express to you half of what is taking place in American secularized schools and culture today. We should celebrate every family, church, and school that is standing as a beacon of hope, light, and absolute truth in this sea of falsehood our children are drowning in.

At RenewaNation, we have discovered that when the family,

church, and school teach God's truth to the children in their care, they become a three-stranded cord that is not easily broken. Our best hope to save our children is to pour God's truth into them all day, every day. If we diligently train them, like these young Hebrew men were trained, God will use them to make a significant difference in our Babylon someday.

THRIVING IN BABYLON WITH MORAL AND SPIRITUAL DEVELOPMENT

As we continue to examine the facts of this account, we are amazed not only by the intelligence and education of these Hebrew young men but also by their moral and spiritual development (Dan. 1:5-16). Nebuchadnezzar wanted to shape these young men into his godless mold by making them violate their moral and biblical commitments to God and His ways. But from a very young age, someone had prepared them to stand at this moment.

It's easy for us to read this biblical account and brush it off, assuming that because they were biblical characters, it must have been easier for them to stand. Nothing could be further from the truth. They were captives in a foreign land where the king killed people on a whim. If you angered him, he would kill you. Life had little value in Babylon. These young men were so well prepared by twelve to fourteen years of age that they were willing to risk everything to be faithful to God.

It also stands out to me that Daniel was so wise at this young age that he could think his way through this and propose a win/win solution to the man responsible for their well-being and development. In Daniel chapter 1, we see the first significant pivotal moment in Daniel's journey to being greatly used by God for the rest of his life: "But Daniel resolved that he would not defile himself with the king's food, or with the wine that he drank. Therefore he asked the chief of the eunuchs to allow him not to defile himself (v. 8). 'Test your servants for ten days; let us be given vegetables to eat and water to drink'" (v. 12).

By the time Daniel was a teenager, he had developed so much confidence in God that he was willing to put God to the test in a positive way, influencing the other young men to follow his leadership. The only way these young men were this well-developed in their moral and spiritual judgment was because their parents and others had helped train and disciple them by following God's plan in Deuteronomy.

> "Hear, O Israel: The Lord our God, the Lord is one. You shall love the Lord your God with all your heart and with all your soul and with all your might. And these words that I command you today shall be on your heart. You shall teach them diligently to your children, and shall talk of them when you sit in your house, and when you walk by the way, and when you lie down, and when you rise. You shall bind them as a sign on your hand, and they shall be as frontlets between your eyes. You shall write them on the doorposts of your house and on your gates" (Deut. 6:4-9).

Please listen to me closely. We can only follow this command if we actually ensure that we teach our children God's truth all day, every day. There is no exception made in this powerful commandment that says, "except for when you send them to school for seven hours a day, 180 days a year," or "when they go into their bedroom at night with unlimited access to the internet or TV."

There is little chance God could have used these young men in such a powerful way if they had spent the first twelve years of their lives being trained in the philosophies of Babylon. They were ready because they had been well-trained in God's truth.

THRIVING IN BABYLON WITH GOD'S FAVOR AND BLESSING

Because they were willing to follow only God's plan, these four young men received God's favor and blessing.

> At the end of ten days it was seen that they were better in appearance and fatter in flesh than all the youths who ate the king's food. So the steward took away their food and the wine they were to drink, and gave them vegetables. As for these four youths, God gave them learning and skill in all literature and wisdom, and Daniel had understanding in all visions and dreams. At the end of the time, when the king had commanded that they should be brought in, the chief of the eunuchs brought them in before Nebuchadnezzar. And the king spoke with them, and among all of them none was found like Daniel, Hananiah, Mishael, and Azariah. Therefore they stood before the king. And in every matter of wisdom and understanding about which the king inquired of them, he found them ten times better than all the magicians and enchanters that were in all his kingdom. And Daniel was there until the first year of King Cyrus (Dan. 1:15-21).

Somewhere, these young men had learned a powerful lesson at a very early age. If we want God's divine blessing, we must do God's work in this world in God's way. They had every excuse to compromise their convictions in Babylon but refused to do so, and God showed them tremendous favor.

The rest of Daniel's story is one of continued testing, obedience, and victory. Much later in their lives, these men would face the capstone stories of the lion's den and the refusal to worship the great statue Nebuchadnezzar built. These accounts testify to the fact that they never walked away from their commitment to God despite the trials and tribulations they faced.

Daniel 3:16-18 gives a perfect picture of who we pray the young people in our Christian families, churches, and schools will become.

> Shadrach, Meshach, and Abednego answered and said to the king, "O Nebuchadnezzar, we have no need to answer you in this matter. If this be so, our God whom we serve is able to deliver us from the burning fiery furnace, and he will deliver us out of your hand, O king. But if not, be it known to you, O king, that we will not serve your gods or worship the golden image that you have set up."

Wow! Isn't this exactly who we pray our children and grandchildren will become? What courage, faith, and holy boldness they displayed before the most powerful man on earth! This was almost two decades after their first major test, yet they still stood strong. Their faithfulness led to the following statement and promotion from the most powerful king on earth.

> Nebuchadnezzar answered and said, "Blessed be the God of Shadrach, Meshach, and Abednego, who has

sent his angel and delivered his servants, who trusted in him, and set aside the king's command, and yielded up their bodies rather than serve and worship any god except their own God. Therefore I make a decree: Any people, nation, or language that speaks anything against the God of Shadrach, Meshach, and Abednego shall be torn limb from limb, and their houses laid in ruins, for there is no other god who is able to rescue in this way." Then the king promoted Shadrach, Meshach, and Abednego in the province of Babylon (Dan. 3:28-30).

Notice the words in verse 30: *"Then the king promoted Shadrach, Meshach, and Abednego…"* Far too many Christian parents have compromised with the world in order to help their children reach a certain level of success in education, business, and sports. We think that by fudging a little here and there, we can get our kids an academic scholarship, or perhaps they will make it big in sports or some other field. We must realize and embrace the simple fact that we need to train our children to stay true to Christ at all costs, and then He will promote them into the positions He has planned for them.

KEY TAKEAWAYS

- If these young men could be raised to excel in Babylon, we can raise our children to excel in America and the world. We must not believe that it's normal for our children to go astray.
- If we hope to raise young men and women like these, we must pour God's truth into their hearts and minds every day, including every school day.
- If we hope to see our children succeed like these young

men, we must be very intentional in how we are training them. We can't just hope and pray they will be ready.

- If we hope to see them succeed, we must not release them into Babylon until they are fully prepared.
- If we hope to see them succeed, we must help them develop a personal and genuine relationship with Jesus. These boys were totally convinced for themselves; they weren't living on their parents' faith.
- If we will do our best, God will do the rest. He will bless them and allow them to make a significant difference for Him and His glory.

God can and will take our children places we could never take them. Most importantly, if we lead them to Christ and teach them to love Him more than anything else in this world, they will ultimately fulfill His plans for their lives. At the end of the day, that should be parents' greatest hope and dream for their children.

SECTION 2

Six Reasons Why We
Must Give Our Children
and Grandchildren a
Biblical Worldview

CHAPTER 4

Children Are Gifts From God and Belong to Him

"Behold, children are a heritage from the Lord, the fruit of the womb a reward. Like arrows in the hand of a warrior are the children of one's youth. Blessed is the man who fills his quiver with them! He shall not be put to shame when he speaks with his enemies in the gate."

Psalm 127:3-5

We must give our children and grandchildren a biblical worldview because our children are gifts from God, and they ultimately belong to Him. God has entrusted parents, grandparents, pastors, and educators with the responsibility of raising the children He created and placed in our care. We will stand before Him someday and give an account of how we stewarded the lives of these precious children. He will not be most concerned with their level of education or athletic achievement. He will ask us, "Did you lead them to know, love, and serve me with all their heart, mind, soul, and strength?"

At the end of the day, if our kids make it to Harvard but don't make it to heaven, we have failed. If they make it to the NBA but die without knowing Jesus, their lives will have been wasted. If they earn millions of dollars and live a glamorous lifestyle but don't place their trust in Christ for salvation and follow Him, they will have failed miserably. All of these things can be a part of our kids' lives, but only if Christ is supreme to them. Otherwise, they will worship something or someone other than the one true God of heaven, and we will have failed at managing the trust God has given us.

God specially designed the family for the rearing and nurturing of children. He wants young men and women to get married, have children, and raise them to become godly offspring (Mal. 2:13-15; Deut. 6:6-9; Prov. 22:6). The best evangelism and discipleship program in the world is the family—dads and moms having children and teaching them God's truth from their earliest days of understanding. We should long to bring them into the world and always see them as gifts from His kind hands. God loves children, and we should, too!

As part of the ungodly system surrounding us today, the dislike of children is one of the most egregious sins of young adults. We now have an entire group of young married people who call themselves DINKS, an acronym for "Dual Income, No Kids."[1] These young people have entire social media groups dedicated to celebrating their unbiblical view of the family and children. They talk about the things they're able to do without the "inconvenience" of children and post pictures of themselves on cruises and in other exotic places around the world. They boast about their nice homes and cars and all the fun they have without the "burden" of children in their lives.

Despite what seems so attractive to these narcissistic young people, this worldview doesn't actually work out well in the long run. First, children and grandchildren bring more joy and blessing into our lives than almost any other thing on earth. I can't imagine the emptiness I would feel if my children and grandchildren were suddenly not in my life. From their earliest days, our daughters have encouraged, inspired, and brought absolute delight to us as parents. Now, our grandchildren light up our lives on a daily basis. Second, God designed children to care for their parents as they age. As I write this book, my brother is caring for our parents in a beautiful apartment he has in his house. All of us kids pitch in and help in any way we can. I currently have a 900-square-foot apartment in my backyard for the primary purpose of caring for my mother-in-law.

Beautiful things come into our lives and world when we truly believe children are a gift from God and embrace His good design of having children and raising them to know, love, and serve Him. All other unbiblical worldviews end up hurting children and, ultimately, society.

REAL-WORLD CONSEQUENCES

Significant amounts of data show the devaluing of children and the abandonment of God's good design of the family in our society today. Young people are waiting longer and longer to get married or avoid marriage altogether. Men get married at a median average age of 30.2, while women marry at 28.4.[2] After getting married, couples are more likely to wait longer to have their first child, and couples are having fewer children than ever before. According to Census data, the number of childless households in the U.S. rose to 43% in 2022, a 7% increase from 2012.[3]

In order to maintain a population, countries must have a total fertility rate (TFR) of 2.1 children per woman capable of giving birth.[4] The birth rate in the United States has now dropped to a new record low of 1.6%—"the lowest rate recorded since the government began tracking it in the 1930s."[5] Strangely, one of the world's lowest and highest fertility rates is in the European Union.[6] While non-Muslims are not having enough children to sustain their population, European Muslims have an average of one more child per woman than other Europeans.[7]

Among the world's population, Muslims are expected to increase by 70% (from 1.8 billion in 2015 to almost three billion in 2060).[8] Pew Research Center warns, "In the next half century or so, Christianity's long reign as the world's largest religion may come to an end, according to a just-released report that builds on Pew Research Center's original population growth projections for religious groups. Indeed, Muslims will grow more than twice as fast as the overall world population between 2015 and 2060 and, in the second half of this century, will likely surpass Christians as the world's largest religious group."[9]

By 2050, over three-quarters of countries (155 of 204) will lack the fertility rates necessary for long-term population sustainability.[10] By 2100, this figure will rise to 97% to include almost all countries in the world (198 of 204).[11] China is right now experiencing a population crisis due to its one-child policy, which forced millions of women in China to have contraception, sterilization, and abortions.[12] The one-child policy in China has led to an imbalance of genders and a decrease in the number of females of reproductive age, which has resulted in a decline in population and birth rates.[13] In 2017, there were under thirteen births per 1,000 people and thirty-three million more men than women.[14] The ratio imbalance between childbearing males and females because of female infanticide has also led to the rise of sex trafficking, bridal kidnapping of females, and the importation of brides from other countries.[15]

When young people are indoctrinated in unbiblical ways of thinking, the consequences in the real world are devastating. Anytime God's good design is violated, and a biblical worldview is rejected in any area of life, terrible things happen.

HOPE IN THE MIDST OF DARKNESS

Bright spots shine in the midst of this darkness. Several friends from China recently told me something amazing as we talked about the many Christians who now populate China. In the 80s and 90s, revival broke out when many Christians were allowed to teach in China's universities.[16] There are now eighty to one hundred million Chinese Christians.[17] One reason there are so many is that many of the young people who were saved in the university revivals refused to have only one child. It costs them dearly to follow God's good design. One of my Chinese friends had three children and had to pay hefty fines because they had more than one child. Wouldn't it be amazing if the children who were brought illegally into this world by Chinese Christians ended up leading China to abandon their atheistic system and become a nation led by Christians? When we follow God's good design, good things happen.

Thankfully, my parents never got the memo about how fun it was to be childless, and they weren't taught that children are a burden who overpopulate and pollute the planet with their additional carbon footprint. They gave birth to nine children who gave them forty-one grandchildren, and those grandchildren have now given them seventy-five great-grand-children. Today, at nearly eighty years of age, they are constantly thrilled to learn of the impact their children and grandchildren are having for the glory of God. Eight of us nine kids have spent most of our lives in full-time vocational ministry, and our youngest brother spent his life fulfilling God's purposes in the military. My parents' steps have slowed, and their public ministry is rare these days, but their influence and impact have never been greater.

The greatest trust a person could ever be given is the responsibility of a child. Michele and I knew from the first day our girls were born that we would stand before God someday and give an account of how we raised them. We determined from day one that our primary purpose in raising them was to help them come to know, love, and serve Jesus. Because this was our God-given mission, we determined that nothing would ever be allowed to influence their young lives in a way that would work against this mission. We knew there would come a day when we would release them into the world, but we determined not to do that until they were prepared to stand on their own. Today, they stand for Jesus as wives, moms, and influencers in their worlds.

Parents and grandparents, our children are gifts from Almighty God, and He has given us the primary responsibility for their wellbeing and upbringing. Everything in this world is working against our children becoming the men and women God designed them to be. We must do everything we can to help them come to know Christ and all of His truth in this world.

CHAPTER 5

We Want Our Children to Grow Up to Bless Our Hearts, Not Break Them

"The father of the righteous will greatly rejoice; he who fathers a wise son will be glad in him."

Proverbs 23:24

We must give our children and grandchildren a biblical worldview because we want them to grow up to bless our hearts, not break them. Perhaps as soon as you saw the title of this chapter, your heart sank, and you thought about putting down this book. Immediately, you were overwhelmed with negative thoughts and feelings as a wayward son, daughter, grandson, or granddaughter came to your mind. If you're like millions of Christian parents, you have prayed and prayed for your lost children with what often seems like no response from God. They continue to break your heart with beliefs and lifestyles that you know are far from God's good design, but it seems they just can't be reached. Perhaps you think you've failed as a parent, and the last thing you want is for someone to bring up anything that reminds you of your regrets. I encourage you to keep reading until the end of this chapter because I have a word of hope for you.

Now, I'd like to talk specifically to those of you who are currently raising your children. I meet people all the time who tell me they were not intentional about the discipleship and biblical worldview training of their children. They share their remorse about how careless they were with their children's education and the influences they allowed in their children's lives. Often, tears well up in their eyes as they tell me how much they wish they had heard my presentation thirty years ago.

The good news for those of you who are currently raising your children is that you are hearing this all-important message now while your children are still young. I urge you not to take it lightly because this literally involves life and death choices your children will ultimately make in this life and for all eternity. I know people who would give up all of their retirement and live in poverty if it would bring their children back to Christ.

If you lead your children to Christ and help them see all of life through the lens of Scripture, there is a high probability they will follow Christ as adults. Though I am fully convinced of this and urging you to do everything in your power to shape your children's worldview, I must make the following truths very clear. I do not believe there is an absolute guarantee our children will choose a path of righteousness if we give them a biblical worldview. However, it is a sure guarantee that if we do not give them a biblical worldview, the world will shape their worldview, and they will go astray and break our hearts. There is no neutral ground in this universe. Ideas, beliefs, and actions either lead our children toward the truth or away from it.

There was a day when most Americans shared essential Judeo-Christian understandings of the world. Most believed the Bible to be true and that there was a heaven to gain and a hell to shun. Most believed strongly in absolute right and wrong and that the Bible determines morality. Those days are over. Our kids are growing up in a world that has lost its mind, and the enemy is using every possible means to steal our children's minds.

As a young pastor, I encountered a mentality that could be summed up like this: Most kids will sow their wild oats as teenagers and young adults but return to the faith and church when they have children. Even though this was a horrible way of thinking, this was often true when families, churches, and society still embraced a mostly biblical view of the world. The young people of those days generally believed the Bible was true and Christ was the only hope for eternal life. Families and churches would lose a young person's heart, but since they still had their heads, these young people would eventually come back to the faith.

These days, with education and pop culture entirely rejecting a biblical worldview, a large majority of young people no longer come back to the faith. A research project from Barna Group found that "nearly three out of every five young Christians (59%) disconnect either permanently or for an extended period of time from church life after age fifteen."[1]

After thousands of faith-busting hours of false teaching, they simply no longer see the need for faith or church. You can lose a child's heart, but if they still believe the truth in their mind, they will most often come back. However, they often never return to the faith once you lose their heart *and* mind.

This is illustrated in the tens of thousands of churches today that are on the verge of extinction. One Easter, the church I attend sent out almost one hundred people to help nine dying churches have a good Easter Sunday. We sent preachers, worship leaders, and singers because these small churches had long ago ceased to keep their young people. If we want our children to grow up and celebrate Easter with us, love the Christ we love, and live the beautiful life He gave us, we must be highly intentional about teaching them God's truth. If we want them to raise our grandchildren to know, love, and serve Christ, we must do everything possible to make this a reality. There is no room for passivity in the rearing of children today.

The late Michael Catt said, "Whoever wants the next generation the most will get them."[2] The devil is passionate about capturing the hearts and minds of our children. With the help of the Holy Spirit, we must be much more passionate than our enemy in leading this generation to Christ. Statistics show that if we are diligent about instilling a biblical worldview in the hearts and minds of our children and grandchildren, a vast majority of them will grow up to bless our hearts, not break them.

A MESSAGE OF HOPE

We all bear a burden for wayward and lost family members, but there is hope. In my family, eight of the nine children have spent most of the last thirty years in vocational Christian ministry. However, one of our brothers decided to take a path away from the Lord for many years. We all longed for him to return home, but it was especially heartbreaking for our parents. The pain of this experience cannot be put into words as we watched him travel the world in the military, and we prayed he would not be taken out of this world unprepared to meet the Lord. By the grace of God, my brother eventually surrendered his life to Christ.

Many of you reading this book have stories to tell that are far more troubling than ours. Through my years as a pastor, numerous elderly saints would say, "Pastor, I'm about to leave this world, and I think I'm the only one who really prays for my lost loved ones. Who's going to pray for them when I'm gone?" I was always so happy to encourage them with the truth that every prayer they had prayed for lost family members had been deposited eternally in the heart of a God who never dies. I want to encourage you today that God will continue to answer your prayers long after you are gone. Your wayward child or grandchild will never get away from your prayers. Just think about that!

I've also had the beautiful opportunity to see the end result of many saints' prayers long after those saints were in heaven. After leading many men and women to Christ, I've heard them say, "Oh, how I wish my mother or father could be here right now! The last thing they said to me before they died was, 'My child, please surrender your life to Jesus and trust Him as your Savior. Please meet me in heaven someday.'" If you are praying for lost and wayward children or grandchildren, I encourage you to continue to pray for them, love them, and speak truth to them until your last breath. And then, rest them in the mighty hands of Jesus.

Let me close this chapter by addressing those of you who are still raising your children. I challenge you to go all in with your children. Commit fully and leave nothing to chance. Don't assume your children will love Christ. They need your intentional involvement and supervision of what they are experiencing in your home, church, school, and media to develop a biblical worldview. You do your best, and God will do the rest, and someday your children will bless your heart, not break it.

CHAPTER 6

We Want Our Children to Experience the Joy and Satisfaction That Comes from Living In Harmony with God's Law and Design

"Blessed are those whose way is blameless,
who walk in the law of the Lord!"

Psalm 119:1

We must give our children and grandchildren a biblical worldview because we want them to experience the joy and satisfaction that comes from living in harmony with God's law and design. Christianity has somehow developed a reputation among many unbelievers as a religion filled with do's and don'ts and the killjoy for all of life. Nothing could be further from the truth! I have often told people who were thinking about becoming Christians that all of God's laws are filled with God's love. His laws were put in place to protect us, not restrict us.

Can you imagine how wonderful our world would be if everyone simply obeyed the Ten Commandments? No lying, stealing, adultery, and dishonoring of parents. We wouldn't need many police, armies, and lawyers. When an individual, family, community, or nation follows God's laws—His good and beautiful design for life—it produces peace, productivity, prosperity, and some of the paradise lost in the fall. Following God's way creates human flourishing, which is exactly what God had in mind when He created humans as the crown of all His creation.

Disobedience and disregard for God's design always bring heartache and pain into our world. If you need a crystal clear example, just think about the Israelites throughout history. God rescued them from slavery and bondage in Egypt. He miraculously led them, fed them, and promised them paradise in Canaan, but their hearts were stubborn. They refused to follow God's plan consistently, so they experienced pain and suffering that was completely unnecessary.

Every year, when I read through the Bible, it depresses me to see this pattern repeated over and over again. I want to scream, "Don't you people know what is going to happen if you obey God or if you disobey God?" Then I think about those of us who are alive today. We also know all this, and yet, we often abandon God's plans for our lives. Following God's plan and design always brings blessings in abundance, and ignoring God's plan always brings disaster.

TEACHING CHILDREN GOD'S WAY WORKS BEST

As parents, grandparents, pastors, and educators, we must deeply impress upon our children and grandchildren the fact that God's way always works best in the real world. Our children must believe with all their hearts that the way of the transgressor is hard, but the yoke of Jesus is easy, and His burden is light. Our children must be taught to see and understand that following Jesus is a life of hope, harmony, and beauty, and following the devil and his lies is the path to failure, brokenness, and sadness. We must paint vivid pictures of this reality to them.

Through the years, I have often tried to show my daughters the difference between their grandmother's blessed life and their lost grandfather's difficult life. I have not done this to be disrespectful to their grandfather, but I wanted them to understand that the wages of sin bring death, not only in the next life but also in this life. Their grandmother, who was abandoned by their grandfather when she was in her early thirties, did not have an easy life for many years. She worked in a factory to provide for my wife and her brother. She remained single for forty years, during which she felt loneliness and rejection due to the abandonment she had suffered. However, she soldiered on and stayed close to Jesus, and He gave her peace, joy, and even unexpected financial gifts and other forms of blessings. Their grandfather, who rejected God's plan for his life, has faced habitual unhappiness and difficulties. I made these distinctions very clear to our daughters because I wanted them to believe with all their hearts that God's way is the good way and that the devil's way produces nothing but difficulty and heartache. The Bible is true when it tells us that "the way of the transgressor is hard" (Prov. 13:15 ASV).

When we diligently teach our children and grandchildren the truth of God's Word and help them see all of life through the lens of God's Word, we set them up for a joyous life. We can never take away all the pain and tragedy they will experience as a result of living in a fallen world, but we can help them live under the blessings that come from living in harmony with God's good design.

I've often said that we don't break God's laws; they break us. There are natural laws and creational norms that will cause us much pain should we ignore them. One of God's natural laws is the law of gravity. We all know that whatever goes up must come down. If you were to choose not to believe in the law of gravity and climb to the highest part of the roof of your house and jump off head first to prove your belief, we all know what would happen. No amount of bravado, ignorance, or defiance would change the outcome. You would be injured, or if your head hit the ground first, you'd likely be paralyzed or dead.

God is not sitting up in heaven waiting to zap people who get out of line, but when we disregard either His natural laws or moral laws, we experience suffering and brokenness. He has given us the manual for how life should be lived, and when we follow the instructions, good things happen. When we ignore His instructions, bad things happen.

Even though our children and grandchildren will face sorrow in this fallen world, when they come to know Christ and understand His will for their lives, they will not experience the unnecessary suffering that comes from breaking God's law. If we hope to see our children and grandchildren live beautiful and meaningful lives, we must give them a biblical worldview and lead them to Christ.

CHAPTER 7

We Want to See Our Children Carry the Christian Faith to Future Generations

"Seven out of ten young teens (70%) either reject the existence of Satan or don't know if he exists. This is a major shift from the beliefs of their parents, who may not have given much thought to Satan's existence, but at least a majority of them believe Satan is real. That point of view has not been handed down from one generation to the next."

George Barna[1]

We must give our children and grandchildren a biblical worldview because we want to see them carry the Christian faith to future generations. In Judges 2:7-10, we find a passage of Scripture that is one of the saddest in the Bible. We read: "And the people served the Lord all the days of Joshua, and all the days of the elders who outlived Joshua, who had seen all the great work that the Lord had done for Israel. And Joshua the son of Nun, the servant of the Lord, died at the age of 110 years. And they buried him within the boundaries of his inheritance in Timnath-heres, in the hill country of Ephraim, north of the mountain of Gaash. And all that generation also were gathered to their fathers. *And there arose another generation after them who did not know the Lord or the work that he had done for Israel.*"

Joshua was a mighty man of God who trusted God and experienced His awesome blessing and power in his life and the nation he led. He's one of the most significant leaders in history, yet he could not pass on the faith to the next generation.

All of us have no doubt seen far too many children from Christian families and churches walk away from the faith. Over and over again, I have talked with precious moms, dads, grandmas, and grandpas after a speech, and in tears, they tell me about their children who have abandoned the faith. I could give numerous heartbreaking statistics about the number of churched young people who have left the faith, but I don't have to convince most of you because you have seen this firsthand. Faith can be gone in a family in one generation without a high level of intentionality. Let me share with you an example of this sad reality.

A REAL-LIFE TRAGEDY

I was speaking at the Ronald Reagan Presidential Library in Simi Valley, California, for a biblical worldview educators' conference. At the conclusion, I went to the Los Angeles International Airport to catch a flight back to the East Coast. I noticed on the monitor in the waiting area that I would have an empty seat next to me on the long flight back to Washington, D.C. As I approached my seat, a young man who looked to be about thirty years old was sitting next to the window. Since I had the aisle seat, I looked at him and said, "Well, this is our lucky flight. We have an empty seat between us."

He quickly responded, "I was hoping a naked woman would come and sit with us."

I thought to myself, "Oh boy, this is going to be an interesting flight."

As soon as I plopped down in my seat, he asked, "So, what do you do for a living?"

I kind of reluctantly told him, and he immediately responded, "Oh, so you're a man of faith. Well, I'm a man of facts. I'm an agnostic."

I never want to argue with unbelievers, but I like asking them questions. Since he was convinced he had all the facts, I said, "So, if you have all the facts, tell me how we got here."

He immediately responded, "The Big Bang."

I asked, "Okay, you believe in The Big Bang. Where did all the stuff come from that blew up?"

He thought about it for a minute and then responded, "I heard a mathematician give the formula for that." I asked him what the mathematician's name was. He had no idea, and he obviously did not know the formula.

I looked at him and said, "Actually, I think you have more faith than I do."

He resisted that suggestion, so I continued by saying, "I have my faith in a God who gave us a book, and when I compare that book to reality, it makes tremendous sense. You have your faith in a mathematician whose name you don't even know." This started a two-hour worldview discussion, as he shared many of his false beliefs about Christianity, including his assumption that I hated homosexuals because I was a Christian.

At some point in this intense conversation, he stopped and said, "My grandmother on one side of my family is a Southern Baptist, and my other grandmother is a Mennonite. My name is Matthew Adam." This shocked me.

Since our conversation, I have often imagined the moment these two Christian grandmothers received the phone call that their new grandson had arrived. No doubt they rushed to the hospital to meet this little boy whose mother likely thought so highly of the Scriptures that she named him after two great men in the Bible. I imagine they held this precious little boy in their arms and dreamed of how God would use his life someday. Thirty years later, I sat with him in the back of an airplane as he told me he didn't believe a single thing his grandparents believed.

I wish this heartbreaking story was an isolated experience, but sadly, it is not. This has happened millions of times over the last fifty years in America. Well-meaning Christian families lacked the passion, intentionality, and wisdom to see what was happening with their children. They allowed those who did not share their Christian values unlimited access to the hearts and minds of their children, and these children believed their teachers and pop culture influencers more than they believed their parents and pastors.

The call God has burned into my soul is to help parents change this sad narrative. We can't control every decision our children make. After all, they are born with a sinful nature that leads them to do wrong and follow Satan's lies. However, there is much we can do to expose the enemy's lies and lead them down a path that will help them embrace Christ and His truth.

The days of passive parenting must be over. The days of doing little teaching and training in the home must be over. The days of allowing others who do not share our values to have great influence over and access to the hearts and minds of our children must be over. As Christian parents, we must stand up and say, "By God's grace and help, I will never surrender my children to the plans Satan has for them! I will fight for their souls with every fiber of my being, confident this is God's desire, and depending on Him to lead and help me every step of the way."

CHAPTER 8

We Want to Spend All Eternity With Our Children

"For what does it profit a man to gain the whole world but lose his soul?"

Mark 8:36

We must give our children and grandchildren a biblical worldview because we want to spend all eternity with them. From the first time I held our daughters, Julianna and Heidi, I knew God had allowed us to bring two never-dying souls into this world. At times, this reality produced in me a sense of heaviness as I contemplated the possibility of our daughters choosing to reject Christ. From their earliest days of understanding, I told them Christ was their only hope for eternal life, and if they rejected Him, it would devastate their mother and me and ruin their entire lives and eternal destiny.

God has given us a tremendous responsibility as parents, and sometimes our priorities and devotion to God's call to raise our children for Christ will be tested. I think of when our oldest daughter was voted one of five all-state basketball players in Virginia. Julianna had always been a natural at basketball, and we loved to watch her play in our small Christian school league. She was and is as tough as nails and never expected anything she didn't earn. One summer, Julianna heard a speaker say that you couldn't be great at anything until you had done it 10,000 times, so she decided to spend many late nights after work shooting free throws in the gym, and she stayed with it until she had made all 10,000 shots.

Somewhere on her basketball journey, the AAU teams asked her to join them. We knew this would be a logical next step for her to reach her full potential in basketball. However, as we evaluated their travel schedule, we realized this would require her to miss the Christian summer camps that had played such an important role in her spiritual development. I had determined I would let her play if they would not make her play on Sundays and would allow her to attend these camps. I talked with Julianna and explained the schedule, and my heart was so blessed when I heard her say, "There is no way I'm missing my summer camps."

I hear more and more about parents' obsession with travel ball. Pastors tell me that parents are taking their children out of church, hoping their children will earn a scholarship to college. Some even dream that their children will become professionals and become rich and famous. I'm not saying young people should never play AAU or on travel teams, but when these things become more important than our children's spiritual development, they are out of place and can cause our children to lose their passion and desire for all the right things.

One of my brothers, who is a pastor, told me a heartbreaking story. One Sunday, as his parishioners were leaving the church, a man told my brother that he wouldn't see him for a while because his eleven-year-old son would be playing travel ball on Sundays. My brother casually inquired how many Sundays they would be gone, and the dad said they would be gone for the next twenty-two Sundays. Years later, when this young man was about seventeen years old, his father approached the pastor of student ministries at my brother's church and said there was something wrong with the youth ministry because his son did not want to attend. When we don't give the things of God the highest priority, it is unlikely that our children will value them. What does it profit a man to gain the whole world but lose his soul?

CHRIST ABOVE ALL

Listen up, parents. God created the entire world and all that is in it. He created sports to teach young men and women valuable lessons that help prepare them to live great lives. He is sovereign over every square inch of this universe, including the basketball court, baseball field, and football field. Many prominent athletes who have embraced a biblical worldview are using their platforms to bring glory to God, and I am grateful for them. I am not proposing that children should spend all their time at church or church camp. I am simply asking you to evaluate your priorities and examine what desires you are fostering in your child's heart.

Our children will love the things we love. They will pursue what they know brings us the most joy. We can't afford to aid the devil in his attempt to capture their hearts and minds for the lesser things of this world. As parents, we must make knowing and serving Christ our family's supreme desire and goal. This is why we sent our girls on multiple mission trips overseas to some of the most desperate places on earth. We wanted them to understand the heart of God for all the world and get their eyes off their American teen experience.

I will never forget the day Heidi returned from a trip to Uganda. Her face was alive with excitement as she shared every significant detail of the trip with us. She told us about visiting a Muslim village and being amazed by the opportunity to sit in mud huts and share the gospel of Jesus with Muslims. Many of them even prayed to accept Christ. My heart was overwhelmed with thankfulness that God had given our daughter this priceless opportunity and the desire to share the gospel.

Some parents are tempted to make academics, gymnastics, and many other things an idol in their child's life. Because of their parents' misplaced priorities, some children are so burdened by the pressure that they get physically sick if they don't get an A on a test or fail to place in a competition. Good grades and success in competitions are good and healthy in their rightful place, but helping our children fall deeply in love with Christ must never take a back seat to anything else in this world.

In just a few short years, we will all be in eternity. I can think of no greater success in life than our children and grandchildren joining us there forever. If we want to spend eternity together with our children, we must make Christ our number one priority.

CHAPTER 9

When We Win the Heart and Mind of Just One Child, They Can Change the World

"Borden not only gave away his wealth, but himself, in a way so joyous and natural that it seemed a privilege rather than a sacrifice."

Mary Taylor in William Borden's biography

We must give our children and grandchildren a biblical worldview because when we win the heart and mind of just one child, they can change the world. To look deeper into this sixth reason why we must give them a biblical worldview, we need to reflect on how the evangelical church in America has done in raising children over the last fifty years.

One day, I had the opportunity to speak with George Barna in person, and I asked him what percentage of millennials in America had a biblical worldview. He looked at me and asked, "Do you want to get depressed?" I said no, but I wanted to hear the truth. His latest research showed that of the seventy to eighty million Americans born in the 80s and 90s, only 4% had developed a biblical worldview.[1]

Is it any wonder that the children of those born during this time are the most confused, anxious, suicidal, and desperate children in American history? They have been given little to no anchor to keep them steady. They are like ships tossed around in a terrible storm; whichever way the wind blows, they go. This generation is so untethered to the truth that they are willing to try anything, even things that make no sense whatsoever in the real world. The failure of the evangelical body of believers in America to pass on the Christian faith has been tragic. Our chickens have come home to roost.

Often, someone will approach me at the end of a speech to ask, "Have you heard about the furries in our schools now?" Unfortunately, I must respond, "Yes, I'm hearing about them everywhere." If you're unfamiliar with this term, it describes people who identify as a particular animal. Many schools allow these children to use the bathroom in litter boxes or go around the school barking all day. It's so insane that it's hard to fathom. But if a boy can choose to be a girl and play on the girl's basketball team, why can't a girl choose to be a dog and bark all day long? If our identity is not tied to anything absolute, it makes sense to declare ourselves anything we want to be at any given moment.

HOPE FOR THE FUTURE

Is there any hope for our children today? You had better believe there is hope! Even though the vast majority of young people have rejected the Christian faith, there is a remnant of young men and women who were taught God's truth at a deep level in their families, churches, and schools. These people love Jesus and are advancing His kingdom in every field across the world. When we give children a biblical worldview and lead them to Christ, they can do amazing things!

I think of T.J. He was a young boy trained in a wonderful Christian home and deeply involved in his excellent church when he came to our Christian school to attend for nine years. We had one mission at our school: partner with parents so their children would be prepared to answer the challenges of this godless world no matter where they landed after high school. I personally instructed our lead biblical worldview educator to help our students understand the major lies they would hear in a non-Christian university and how and why the biblical worldview was superior to all other worldviews.

T.J. graduated from our school and went to a non-Christian college. For the first time in nine years, he had a teacher who was anti-Christian, pro-abortion, and opposed to a biblical worldview in every way. This English teacher decided he would have the students debate a variety of subjects on a regular basis. He split the twenty-five students into two groups and asked them to make their case on mostly benign subjects, such as the best restaurants in their city.

The debate teams T.J. was placed on consistently won debate after debate, and the teacher told him he should consider becoming a lawyer because he was that good at debate. I believe he was good because we had taught him absolute truth and the basic principles of logic and rhetoric. T.J. was the only student in the class who had been given a biblical worldview through his family, church, and school.

Things continued to go well for T.J. until the day the teacher announced the subject of that day's debate would be abortion.

T.J. knew the teacher was pro-abortion and watched in fear as twenty-three of the twenty-five students stated they were for abortion and wanted to argue in its favor. T.J. was the only student to stand against abortion. One student didn't know what he believed, but because of T.J.'s history of winning debates, he chose to be on his team.

The teacher instructed the twenty-three students who were pro-abortion to make their case first. I asked T.J. how he felt at that moment, and he said he thought he should have listened a lot more in the worldview classes that had covered this issue. However, the more the pro-abortion group talked, the more T.J. gained confidence because their arguments sounded weak to him. When his turn came, God helped him to make one point after another, showing the reasons why abortion is not good for women, children, and our society at large. He finished his arguments by stating that, in reality, every time a woman had an abortion, a baby was murdered.

As he always did, the teacher looked at the class and said, "If you've changed your minds, switch sides." T.J. was blown away when all twenty-three young men and women came over to his side. It only took one young man, grounded in the truth, to win the hearts and minds of a whole classroom of young people who had never heard the first good argument against abortion.

All across America, God is raising up a new generation of young men and women like T.J. who know the Lord, have a deep understanding of God's truth, and are willing to take it into the arena of ideas. When they do, they excel in business, medicine, law, government, law enforcement, ministry, and more because they have discovered God's good design works out better in the real world more than any other worldview.

SECTION 3

The Fundamental Differences Between Biblical Worldview Education and Secular Worldview Education

CHAPTER 10

The Role of Education In the Worldview Development of Children

"Let us not fool ourselves—without Christianity, without Christian education, without the principles of Christ inculcated into young life, we are simply rearing pagans."

Peter Marshall

In this section, I want to have an open and honest talk with you about the role education plays in the worldview development of children. This may seem like a significant shift in the flow of the book, but it is so important I chose to include this section. There has been a great divide in the evangelical church on education, and I understand how, like no other topic, this one gets Christian parents whose children are attending non-Christian schools fired up. I do not believe you are a bad parent or you don't love your children because your child is in a non-Christian school. Likely, this discussion increases your blood pressure because you truly want to do what is right for your children. Perhaps you wonder if there is a different and better way when someone talks about Christian education.

I have seen people get extremely defensive about this issue. If you are the parent of a public school student or the pastor of a church that promotes enrolling children in public school, I simply ask you to hold your defense for just a bit and hear me out. We must be willing to think long and hard about this issue without shutting off the discussion because nothing less than our children's eternal destiny is at stake. You love your children, God loves your children, and I love your children, so let's talk.

Over the last fifty years, the evangelical church and most families in America assumed everything would be okay if we took our kids to church a couple of times a week and generally guided them in truth at home. We greatly underestimated the influence of media, pop culture, and education and are shocked to hear our kids tell us they no longer believe what we believe.

What are American children believing these days? Prominent researcher and bestselling author Dr. George Barna partnered with the Family Research Council and Arizona Christian University's Cultural Research Center to conduct an extensive study of children aged eight to twelve on their beliefs about the Bible, and the results are deeply troubling.[1]

A significant percentage, 69%, believe that God exists as the all-knowing, all-powerful, perfect Creator and ruler of the universe, but a mere 21% believe the Bible offers a comprehensive and trustworthy understanding of right and wrong.[2]

Just 36% believe the only way to address the consequences of sin is by acknowledging your sins, seeking God's forgiveness through Jesus Christ, and relying on Him for salvation, and slightly less than that, 35%, believe sin is real and severe and that we are all sinners by choice.[3]

Only 27% believe their ultimate purpose in life is fulfilling God's will, just 17% believe success means doing what the Bible teaches, and only 25% trust that the Bible is completely true and relevant to their life.[4]

How have we gotten to this point? Secularized education, blended worldviews, Bible-lite church experiences, and little intentional training in the home have led to generations of children who do not deeply know God and His plans for this world.

When I speak in Northwest and Northeast America, I'm often told the culture has grown so secularized that it's extremely difficult to plant a church or operate a Christian school. A secularized worldview has taken deep root in the hearts of many parents, and they see little to no need to train their children in God's truth.

We can no longer afford to ignore or downplay the role education plays in our children's worldview development, and we cannot keep doing the same thing over and over and expect different results. We must wake up to reality and give this generation of children a biblical worldview, or the entire country will soon become secularized, just like Europe.

Despite the evidence we see every day of our descent into a spiritual dark age, many people continue to argue against Christian education and for placing Christian children in non-Christian schools. The best argument for this is that we need to be salt and light and evangelize those who attend these schools. Again, I see the value of Christian adults serving in this role in non-Christian schools. I have many friends and acquaintances who are doing this as well as it can be done. However, our children are rarely prepared to serve as effective missionaries, and far too many of them end up being evangelized by the lies they hear rather than evangelizing their classmates for Christ. Secularized education is playing a significant role in the loss of faith for evangelical children, but many evangelical pastors and parents continue to push back against this reality.

Again, I believe you love your children and the children in your church with all your heart and want the best for them. So, let's think through this together by considering the vast amount of hours children spend being trained in the worldview of their teachers and curriculum. At 180 days per year for seven hours each day for thirteen years, our children will spend 16,380 hours at school. Surely, we should take a serious look at what they are experiencing in those 16,380 hours and how this impacts how they view the world.

When I did this math at my first pastorate in the inner city of Miami-Fort Lauderdale, Florida, the reality was sobering. All except one out of the one-hundred-plus children in my church attended public schools in Broward County, and many of these young people lived in homes with parents who were recent converts to Christianity. Each week, we had these kids for only about two hours at church while the school had them for thirty-five to forty-five hours! They would tell me about the unbelievable peer pressure they were experiencing to have premarital sex and be involved in many ungodly activities. They asked me, "Pastor, do you realize that everything you teach us at church, they teach us the opposite at school?"

There, in that little inner-city church, I had an epiphany. I saw that if we were going to win the hearts and minds of these children, we would have to gain access to them at a much more significant level. This pivotal moment opened my eyes to the battle that was raging for the souls of our children, and I began to think about how the family, church, and school could best disciple children.

NO WORLDVIEW-NEUTRAL PROGRAMS

We must realize there are no worldview-neutral educational programs. Every school, teacher, and textbook teaches either a biblical view of life or a non-biblical view. I'm not saying everything taught in a non-Christian school is unbiblical. However, every teacher has a specific set of core beliefs that influence how they teach the curriculum to their students, and every textbook is written by someone with a set of beliefs that shape the text. The Bible says in Luke 6:40, "A disciple is not above his teacher, but everyone when he is fully trained will be like his teacher."

Let me pause here to say that I am deeply grateful for all the Christian teachers and administrators serving as missionaries in public schools. In no way do I want to discourage you because you are making a needed and significant difference in the calling God has given you. You are a bulwark against much of the evil being propagated, and I know your work is highly challenging these days.

At the same time, we must realize that every school teaches doctrine because every school teaches children what to believe. All schools indoctrinate children at some level, and the only question is: *What doctrines are they indoctrinating children with?* At school, children learn about origins, history, our purpose for being here, what the rules are and who makes them, where we go when we die, and who the heroes are.

I firmly believe you can shape a child's entire belief structure simply by telling them who the heroes and villains are. For example, if a teacher believes racist bigots founded America, that teacher will teach American history much differently than a teacher who believes God used America's imperfect founders to build the most prosperous, just, and productive government structure in the history of the world. Many of America's young people hate America today because they have read textbooks that denigrate our country, have been taught by teachers who despise America, and have never been told there is another side to the story.

Since all schools tell children a big story or meta-narrative about life, they share what they believe about God's place in this world. When God is never connected to the study of math, science, history, English, business, medicine, law, or any other subject, children begin to assume that God is only relevant to church-related things like Bible reading and worship music but irrelevant to all other aspects of life. This is why so many do not trust the Scriptures as authoritative in all areas of life and sufficient for all things. A great Christian education in the family, church, and school helps children connect all of life to the One who created all things and to the ultimate purposes for which all things have been created (Col. 1:16).

Secularized education—education that has been stripped of God's truth—produces young people who have no idea how God relates to the real world, even though they may still attend church and trust Jesus as their Savior. Some call this the Sacred/Secular Divide (SSD), and I believe it is one of the most significant curses in evangelical Christianity.[5] SSD is the reason many Christians stay out of areas like politics and why the largest churches in history exist in major cities that are rotting from within. They see certain things as existing in a realm beyond the reach of God's work in this world when, in reality, no area is beyond God's reach.

God's truth speaks to every area of our lives. If we want our children to hold fast to His Word and stand firmly for Christ in a godless culture, we must take seriously the role education plays in their worldview development.

CHAPTER 11

What Is the Purpose of Education?

"Isolating the student from large sections of human knowledge
is not the basis of a Christian education. Rather, it is giving
him or her the framework for total truth, rooted in the Creator's
existence and in the Bible's teaching, so that in each step of
the formal learning process, the student will understand
what is true and what is false and why it is true or false."

Francis Schaeffer

In the coming chapters, we'll examine the purpose of education and how a genuinely biblical education teaches children God's truth in all areas of study and helps students understand their purpose in life. By asking some of life's major questions that all educational systems attempt to answer, we'll compare and contrast several fundamental differences between what children learn in a biblical worldview education and a secularized worldview education.

QUESTION: WHAT IS THE PURPOSE OF EDUCATION?

BIBLICAL WORLDVIEW EDUCATION ANSWER:	SECULARIZED WORLDVIEW EDUCATION ANSWER:
The purpose of education is to lead children to know the one true God and develop their knowledge, talents, skills, and character so that they can take dominion of the earth and, by doing so, show the world God's beauty and glory.	The goal of education is the transmission of knowledge and skills that will prepare young people to go to college, get a job, and become productive members of society.

You will notice similarities between the two definitions given here for the purpose of education, but in the secularized definition, essential things are left out that can never be taught in most non-Christian schools. A truly Christian, biblical worldview education will show children how God views everything from the proper role of government, economics, law enforcement, and more. This scriptural foundation for the purpose of education is shown in 2 Corinthians 10:4-5: "For the weapons of our warfare are not of the flesh but have divine power to destroy strongholds. We destroy arguments and every lofty opinion raised against the knowledge of God, and take every thought captive to obey Christ."

We want to train a new generation of young people to be prepared to bring every thought in every field of study under the Lordship of Jesus Christ. In order for our children to be able to do this, they must be exceptionally educated.

John Gresham Machen said, "A Christian boy or girl can

learn mathematics, for example, from a teacher who is not a Christian; and truth is truth, however learned. But while truth is truth, however learned, the bearing of truth, the meaning of truth, the purpose of truth, even in the sphere of mathematics, seem entirely different to the Christian from that which they seem to the non-Christian; and that is why a truly Christian education is possible only when Christian conviction underlies not a part but all of the curriculum of the school."[1] Secularized schools can never show children the truth of God's involvement in all areas of study; therefore, they can never give a child a truly holistic education. So much truth is left out of secularized education.

Let me give you a few examples of what I mean by seeing God's involvement in everything. One of the fundamental differences in teaching from a biblical perspective is the goal of helping students understand the *why* behind what is being taught. The *why* is the crucial element in how biblical worldview education teaches subjects differently than a secularized worldview education.

Take language arts, for example. How would a biblical worldview education teach language arts differently than a secularized education? Aren't there just nouns, verbs, and pronouns? Isn't grammar just grammar? Why should students work diligently to master reading, writing, and speaking? The biblical worldview answers this question by recognizing that humans are created in the image of God and, therefore, have abilities that no other species possess. Reading, writing, and speaking are three amazing communication skills God gave only to humans. God is a speaking and writing God, and He chose to pass on those abilities to us. We should consider it a tremendous privilege and honor to possess these skills. Since these abilities are truly unique in what they allow us to do and are a part of what it means to have God's image stamped upon us, we should have a great desire to develop them to their highest capacity so we can use them to take dominion of the earth and bend it back toward God's original design.

I stated this in the last chapter, but I want to repeat it because it's so important. When a child spends thirteen years in a school where God is never connected to any relevant part of the world, such as business, medicine, law, government, history, math, and science, children naturally begin to assume God is only involved in what happens at church and uninvolved in the rest of life. This Sacred/Secular Divide (SSD) is why many Christians are afraid of bringing Christianity into the public square; they were convinced through their education that Christianity is acceptable as long as it stays in the private world.

Most children who attend non-Christian schools don't become atheists—they become secularists who see Christ as relevant to only a narrow part of life. The reality is that Christ is sovereign over every ounce of this universe and has a good design for how everything should operate. When we show children His excellent design for all of life and unleash them into their area of calling, God's kingdom is built, and the world sees God's beauty and glory.

CONNECTING GOD'S WORK IN EVERY SUBJECT

Let's look at another example of how showing God's hand in everything can only be experienced in a biblical worldview educational setting. A student tells their teacher, "I strongly desire to become a homebuilder, but I want to do something for God, not just work to make money." The student who lives with a Sacred/Secular Divide is not able to connect God's work in this world to homebuilding and thinks that one should become a missionary or pastor in order to do God's work.

A teacher with a biblical worldview would show this student that building homes for people is part of restoring what is broken in this world and, therefore, is God's work. They would explain that Adam and Eve had no need for shelter in the Garden of Eden before the fall because without sin there would have been no threat of violent storms, robbery, or physical attacks. But after the fall, Adam and Eve were cast out of the garden into a world now filled with evil. They couldn't even sleep at night without fear of harm from people and wild animals. To rectify this problem and restore a small amount of the paradise they lost from the fall, they took dominion of the earth by building shelters out of trees and stone.

Today, when a young man or woman feels a call to build buildings, they are bending creation back toward God's original design of safety and security for humans. By sheltering people, they are doing God's work of loving their neighbor and creating human flourishing through the safety and comfort a home can provide. The biblical worldview answer will free this student to follow God's call in homebuilding and bring deep purpose to their work. This kind of holistic teaching can never be given in a non-Christian school setting because a secular educator and curriculum cannot answer students' questions from a biblical worldview perspective.

In many cases today, young people hate going to school because the true purpose of education has never been made real to them. In most secular school settings, they don't see the connection between education and God's grand plans for them and the world. Children are told they must study math, science, and other subjects to get a job and make money, but that's simply not a compelling enough reason to make them hungry to learn. As soon as they have developed the minimal skills to get a job, many don't see why they should continue to be subjected to hour after hour of learning in a classroom because they don't understand the ultimate purpose of education.

John Milton said, "The end then of learning is to repair the ruins of our first parents by regaining to know God aright, and out of that knowledge to love him, to imitate him, to be like him, as we may the nearest by possessing our souls of true virtue, which being united to the heavenly grace of faith makes up the highest perfection."[2] Wherever education has been secularized, including in some Christian schools and homeschools, children will not have an understanding of God's purpose for education. Secularized education, whether private or public, offers the wrong answers to all the major questions of life.

Only a biblical worldview education trains students to take every thought captive to obey Christ and destroy every argument and lofty opinion raised against the knowledge of God. Unless we teach students to see God's hand in everything, they will graduate with little understanding of who they are and what their purpose in life is.

The RenewaNation Education Advancement Program (REAP) offers multiple ways to support you in biblically educating children. Reap.renewanation.org, our Christian education website, hosts numerous articles and resources, such as training videos and courses, to encourage, inspire, and equip you with biblical worldview education instructional and mentoring techniques. We also offer a complete launch program with dedicated coaches to assist churches and parents with starting Christian schools. Additionally, we provide homeschooling guidance and support to help you and your family undertake what can be an enriching, life-changing journey. REAP's multiple biblical worldview education offerings serve as a powerful and transformative source for the discipleship of children and young adults.

CHAPTER 12

Who Has Ultimate Authority In This World?

"It is a fact that unless children are brought up in the nurture and admonition of the Lord, they, and the society which they constitute or control, will go to destruction. Consequently, when a state resolves that religious instruction shall be banished from the schools and other literary institutions, it virtually resolves on self-destruction."

Charles Hodge

We are witnessing a crisis of authority in the world today. Children and young people are disrespectful at levels never before seen and often despise any form of authority. Our inner cities are out of control. Stores are forced to lock up the most basic items since cities have decided not to prosecute crimes like theft. All of us are paying more for insurance, groceries, and just about everything else because some refuse to submit to the laws of our land. Rebellious people make for a very bad society, and wrongly answering the foundational question of who has ultimate authority in the world has created chaos.

QUESTION: WHO HAS ULTIMATE AUTHORITY IN THIS WORLD?

BIBLICAL WORLDVIEW EDUCATION ANSWER:	SECULARIZED WORLDVIEW EDUCATION ANSWER:
Since God created all things and clearly laid out His will for our lives and world, we are accountable to Him and will give a full account of our lives someday.	Man is autonomous, and there is no higher power to whom we are accountable. We rule our own universe and destiny.

Secularized education fails miserably in the answer to this most basic and fundamental question of who has ultimate authority. Now, don't misunderstand me. Secularized schools are not overtly teaching children to disobey their parents or break into stores. However, by not teaching the truth that there is a God to whom we will answer, secularized education undermines all other earthly authority God has placed to help create order, security, and flourishing, such as parents, grandparents, teachers, and government officials. The chaos we see directly results from not understanding and respecting God as the ultimate authority.

From the first words of the Bible, we see God's complete authority: "In the beginning, God created…" (Gen. 1:1). God gives us these powerful truths in His Word: "The fear of the Lord is the beginning of wisdom, and the knowledge of the

Holy One is insight" (Prov. 9:10), and "The fear of the Lord is the beginning of knowledge; fools despise wisdom and instruction" (Prov. 1:7). The foundation of all educational systems should be a holy fear of Almighty God. This fear causes humans to bow reverently before Him and listen to what He has to say. It leads people to follow His good design and submit to His plans. Only in a Christian educational setting can a child be taught the proper fear of the Lord.

INFLUENCES IN WORLDVIEW FORMATION

When it was time for my wife and me to educate our daughters, my experience in my first pastorate led us to reflect deeply on how we could best guide our children to embrace God's ideas in every aspect of their lives. God unexpectedly uprooted me from the church in South Florida and led me to take a pastorate in Virginia. When I asked in a church board meeting which Christian school was the best to enroll my daughter in, I received a surprising response. One board member, who I discovered was also a county board of supervisors member, asked me, "Why would you waste your money on a Christian school?" He told me that the public schools in our area were practically Christian because they were filled with Christian administrators and teachers. I was grateful to hear this, and as a thirty-two-year-old dad, I was willing to give them a look.

My wife and I visited the local elementary school to speak with the administrator. This rural school had many Christian teachers. However, the administrator who spoke with me wore New Age symbols as earrings, and within a few minutes, I quickly realized she did not have a biblical worldview. She informed me they would offer sex education to my second grader but couldn't provide the material for me to preview.

She assured me that if I wanted to opt my daughter out of the sex education class, I could do that. As I was thinking about this, I realized that even if my daughter didn't attend the sex education class, the students who did would likely share what they had learned with her throughout the school year.

On that day, I made a final decision on how we would educate our daughters. I looked at my wife as we walked out of that school and said, "I will never allow someone who doesn't share our values and worldview to have access to the minds of our daughters until they are mature enough to defend the truth." We were not perfect parents, but we are so grateful to God to have two adult daughters who love the Lord, married strong Christian men, and are raising our grandchildren to know Jesus. We do not doubt that the godly teachers and curriculum our daughters interacted with helped shape their worldview and encouraged them to surrender their lives to Jesus.

Teachers, curriculum, and classmates play a significant role in forming our children's worldviews and will either dissuade or encourage their ultimate decision to surrender their lives to Jesus and His way. We must realize that unless God's truth undergirds every subject, His authority is being undermined directly or indirectly. Biblical curriculum and godly teachers who share our biblical values and worldview will help our children grow up to know, love, and serve Jesus and accept Him as the ultimate authority on all matters of life.

CHAPTER 13

Where Did We Come From?

"In the beginning was the Word, and the Word was with God, and the Word was God. He was in the beginning with God. All things were made through him, and without him was not any thing made that was made."

John 1:1-3

Genesis 1:1 says, "In the beginning, God created the heavens and the earth." There are profound implications when children are not taught the true origin of the universe and life. If we cannot correctly answer the question of where we come from, we cannot answer why we are here. The purpose and meaning of life are lost when we do not answer the question of origins from a biblical perspective.

QUESTION: WHERE DID WE COME FROM?

BIBLICAL WORLDVIEW EDUCATION ANSWER:	SECULARIZED WORLDVIEW EDUCATION ANSWER:
By His almighty power and the brilliance of His creative mind, God created and designed everything in the universe and created humans in His own image.	Billions of years ago, the universe originated without a designer, expanding from a dense, hot state into its present form, and humans evolved to where we are today.

The most commonly held secularized view of origins taught in America's non-Christian schools today teaches children that we are cosmic accidents with no ultimate purpose except the survival of the species. When we attempt to explain life and the universe apart from God, there are countless negative consequences, such as removing from children their obligation to be accountable to God.

George Barna discusses some of these serious implications in his book *Raising Spiritual Champions*. He shares what thirteen- and fourteen-year-olds believe about God and our origins: "...barely one-third of newly minted teens (36%) believe that God exists and is the all-knowing, all-powerful Creator of the universe, who is perfect and just, and who rules the universe today. In contrast, closer to half (43%) are *Don'ts*—people who don't know if there is a God, don't believe in His existence, or don't care one way or the other."[1] Only 27% believe that God is the source of all truth as revealed in the Bible, and just 18% turn to God and His teachings for guidance on morality.[2]

Barna writes, "A large share believes that there are no

absolute moral truths that are impervious to conditions and personal preferences. Among the many consequences of that point of view is the dismissal of the idea of sin, the rejection of the notion that Jesus Christ is the only means to eternal salvation, the repudiation of the Bible as a source of inerrant truth principles for everyone, and the denial that morality is predictable and consistent."[3]

In a post on X, Nancy Pearcey further points out the consequences of the secular view of origins, quoting Marvin Minsky in his book *The Society of the Mind*: "Scientists cannot live out the materialist worldview they profess: *'The brain is nothing but a three-pound computer made of meat.'* Computers do not have free will, so the implication is that neither do we. And yet… *'No matter that the physical world provides no room for freedom of will; that concept is essential to our models of the mental realm.'* We cannot *'ever give it up.'* Thus, *'we're virtually forced to maintain that belief, even though we know it's false.'"*[4]

Free will cannot be reconciled within the materialist worldview because it doesn't recognize the problem in the world as sin and the solution as Christ. God grants us free will, which we are to exercise within the laws He has set up. When children are taught they are nothing more than evolutionary creatures not created with any real purpose, it creates the rampant confusion we see today. If we are simply highly evolved animals, we can make our own rules, so why not allow children to determine their gender, family structure, and sexual preference? This type of thinking results from a secularized worldview of where we came from.

SCIENCE FOR THE GLORY OF GOD

Because of the Sacred/Secular Divide, many believe a

Christian view of origins is incompatible with science, but that could not be further from the truth. Far from being anti-science, a biblical worldview of creation gives students an ultimate reason to pursue the discovery of all God has made. Many of the first great scientists happened to be Christians who were highly motivated to discover how God's universe works in order to take dominion of it for His glory and create human flourishing. Nancy Pearcey and Charles Thaxton write in *The Soul of Science: Christian Faith and Natural Philosophy*, "The earlier scientist was very likely to be a believer who did not think scientific inquiry and religious devotion incompatible. On the contrary, his motivation for studying the wonders of nature was a religious impulse to glorify the God who had created them."[5] God is "the Alpha and the Omega, the first and the last, the beginning and the end" (Rev. 22:13), and if we are to understand our origins, we must begin with God.

The biblical worldview teaches students to look properly at the origins of the world and humanity by starting with God, who created all things in His power and wisdom and designed the world to function in certain ways. When students see the beauty of the world and start to understand the deep complexities involved, their hearts are naturally drawn to worship and adore the Creator God. They bow in reverence before the One who has the power and ability to create something so magnificent. A God who could create and hold the vast universe together is surely a God who should be loved and trusted.

CHAPTER 14

What Does It Mean to Be Human?

"So God created man in his own image, in the image of God he created him; male and female he created them."

Genesis 1:27

The question of what it means to be human is a complex and enduring one that people have asked for thousands of years. What sets humans apart from other species in the world? Why do humans desire to live a life of meaning and significance while all other creatures seek simply to survive? To understand humanity's unique value, we must understand what it truly means to be human.

QUESTION: WHAT DOES IT MEAN TO BE HUMAN?

BIBLICAL WORLDVIEW EDUCATION ANSWER:	SECULARIZED WORLDVIEW EDUCATION ANSWER:
Humans were created in God's image as eternal souls with unique abilities given to us by God that make us superior and more valuable than anything else.	Humans are animals that evolved to have more abilities than other animals but possess no inherent rights, privileges, or value above other species and the planet.

In a secularized worldview education, children are taught that we are nothing more than evolved animals with no special rights or privileges who pollute the planet and rob other species of their rightful place. When children learn in non-Christian schools that "humans are one type of several living species of great apes" and that we "evolved alongside orangutans, chimpanzees, bonobos, and gorillas,"[1] they will not understand their unique value as image-bearers of God.

Our failure to teach children the truth about what it means to be human has created all kinds of serious problems. Many people today overvalue animals and greatly undervalue human life. Hollywood is filled with people fighting to save whales and pets in shelters while also fighting for women to be able to kill their babies up to the moment of birth. Young couples choose not to have children in a misguided effort to "save the planet." These people have never been taught the truth about what it actually means to be a human in God's world, and as a result, they significantly devalue human life.

THE PROPER VALUE OF HUMAN LIFE

The biblical worldview has brought more value to human life than any other worldview. In biblical worldview educational settings, we teach children not to abort the life of a baby in the womb or euthanize a person because to kill an image-bearer of God is an assault against God Himself. In Genesis 9:6, God said, "Whoever sheds the blood of man, by man shall his blood be shed, for God made man in his own image."

In many countries today, there are minimal sentences for heinous crimes like murder. The average sentence length for homicide in France is just 6.1 years![2] Why would countries impose such lenient sentences for such egregious crimes? Because, in a secularized worldview, humans are simply animals with no soul. How could we hold people accountable for their actions if we are only animals living out animal instincts? If we deviate from commonly accepted norms, it's simply viewed as humans giving into their lower instincts and not immoral in the real sense of the word. If we are just highly evolved animals driven and predetermined by our chemical makeup, it's hard to declare that evil actually exists.

In a biblical worldview, humans are held to a much higher standard. We are created in God's image as intellectually, morally, and socially superior to all other species. The tremendous privileges and special abilities given to us by God to think, design, plan, speak, write, and read create a unique level of accountability for humans. God commands us to live according to His good design and ultimate code of morality. We have the responsibility to know, love, and serve Him or the ability to choose to reject Him. If we fail to live up to His standards or deny Him, we face consequences in this life and the next. Through Christ and the power of the Holy Spirit,

God has made it possible for humans to know and obey Him.

When our children are taught a biblical worldview of what it means to be human, they will place the proper value on God's creation and live mindfully of His design and priorities. A genuine Christian education will help them understand God's good design for humanity and the world.

CHAPTER 15

What Is Our Purpose In Life?

"The end then of learning is to repair the ruins of our first parents by regaining to know God aright, and out of that knowledge to love him, to imitate him, to be like him, as we may the nearest by possessing our souls of true virtue, which being united to the heavenly grace of faith makes up the highest perfection."

John Milton

I'll never forget riding down the road with my dad when I was a boy. He would reach over, pat me on the leg, and say, "Son, you are destined for leadership in the kingdom of God. Never let the devil destroy or distract you from the mission God has for you." By God's grace, my godly parents drilled into the hearts and minds of their children that the number one reason for our existence was to know, love, serve, and glorify Christ. What our children are taught about their purpose matters and greatly affects the course of their lives.

QUESTION: WHAT IS OUR PURPOSE IN LIFE?

BIBLICAL WORLDVIEW EDUCATION ANSWER:	SECULARIZED WORLDVIEW EDUCATION ANSWER:
Our purpose is to glorify God by loving Him fully and loving our neighbor as ourselves, by ruling well over His creation, and by making disciples of Jesus Christ.	Your purpose is to do whatever brings you happiness and fulfillment and to preserve the planet, animals, and other living organisms.

In secularized worldview education, children are taught to discover whatever brings them personal satisfaction and do whatever it takes to make themselves happy. The focus for education, college, career, and life is geared toward self. I recall a plane flight where I sat next to an eighteen-year-old German girl visiting the United States for the first time. Thankfully, she spoke excellent English, and we had a wonderful conversation. I asked her what kind of schools she had attended in Germany, and she said her entire school life was spent in German public schools. When I asked what she had been taught about her purpose in life, she didn't hesitate for a second. She said, "They taught me the purpose of life is to do whatever I want to do." I asked, "Would it be accurate to say they taught you that the purpose of life was to do whatever you want to do in order to make yourself happy?" She responded, "That's exactly what they taught me."

When young people across the world are taught in secularized education to do whatever it takes to make themselves happy, is it any wonder that so many are living aimless and unfulfilled lives? Most are simply pursuing the next pleasure that will bring them a measure of temporary happiness. Ultimately, this leaves young people in a state of perpetual unhappiness, trapped by addictions and the chase for the next quick fix.

One of the most important things we must do as we train children in the family, church, and school is to help connect them to God's grand purpose for their lives. When you talk to many young people today about their plans and dreams, there is a distinct lack of purpose. Because our culture has convinced them that personal pleasure and so-called happiness are life's goals, too many young people are not living for causes greater than themselves. I think one of the reasons we call the World War II generation the greatest generation in American history is because so many of them were taken to the brink of death during the war and were forever connected to a life-and-death cause that was greater than their own personal aspirations. When we look at the Scriptures, we are given a grand purpose for life, summarized by the following three key commands.

THE CREATION OR DOMINION MANDATE

"Be fruitful and multiply and fill the earth and subdue it, and have dominion over the fish of the sea and over the birds of the heavens and over every living thing that moves on the earth" (Gen. 1:28).

God has called humans to rule well over His created order. We are His vice-regents on earth. After the fall, it became more difficult to rule the earth, but the mandate stayed the same.

We must inspire our young people to manage this planet well. Now that we deal with the effects of the fall, we must, as John Milton put it, "Repair the ruins of our first parents."[1] Christ redeems us individually so that we can become restorers of the brokenness in this world. I like to say we are called to bend creation back toward God's original design. With this understanding, all legitimate professions become God's work, and each young person should be challenged to discover what role they are called to play in managing the world God has given us.

THE GREAT COMMANDMENT

> *"But when the Pharisees heard that he had silenced the Sadducees, they gathered together. And one of them, a lawyer, asked him a question to test him. 'Teacher, which is the great commandment in the Law?' And he said to him, 'You shall love the Lord your God with all your heart and with all your soul and with all your mind. This is the great and first commandment. And a second is like it: You shall love your neighbor as yourself. On these two commandments depend all the Law and the Prophets'"* (Matt. 22:34-40).

If we want our young people to experience deep meaning and purpose in life, we must help them understand that loving God supremely and other people deeply are the key elements of a rich and beautiful life. It wasn't until I was twenty-two years old that I fell in total love with Jesus and others. This experience changed the whole trajectory of my life. Until this experience, I had been seeking and searching but never quite finding the ultimate purpose of my life. Once my heart was fully yielded to and in love with Christ, He showed me what my role would be in restoring this broken world. The ultimate cause that is greater than ourselves is the cause of Christ. When our young people connect with this cause, they will be willing to sacrifice everything in order to see His will be done on earth as it is in heaven.

THE GREAT COMMISSION

"Go therefore and make disciples of all nations, baptizing them in the name of the Father and of the Son and of the Holy Spirit, teaching them to observe all that I have commanded you. And behold, I am with you always, to the end of the age" (Matt. 28:19-20).

No matter what area of creation renewal God calls a young person into, we must help them understand that every human being they come in contact with will have a never-dying soul. They must also understand that at the core of redeeming this broken world is Christ's plan to redeem lost and sinful human beings. We will not be able to rule well over God's created order unless vast numbers of people have allowed Jesus to deal with the sin issue deep within their hearts. Sin entered this world, and it has been humanity's number one problem ever since. Every Christian must recognize that unless we share the gospel and lead men and women to Christ, our greatest efforts at "repairing the ruins of our first parents" will be futile.

Any form of non-Christian education will fail to plant this grand purpose in the souls of our children. When we connect our young people to God's purposes for their lives, they will soon begin to live with a life vision that allows them to meet the challenge we received from the great missionary William Carey, who said, "Expect great things from God, attempt great things for God."[2]

CHAPTER 16

How Do We Determine Identity and Gender?

"You are the result of the attentive, careful, thoughtful, intimate, detailed, creative work of God. Your personality, your sex, your height, your features, are what they are because God made them precisely that way."

James Hufstetler

You might have noticed that most of our biblical worldview answers are found in the first few chapters of the Bible. Genesis is foundational in so many ways to the biblical worldview. It's hard to believe that it is necessary to ask and answer how we determine identity and gender, but as our world has strayed further from God's truth, we are dealing with more absurdity every day. This question is front and center in almost all non-Christian educational settings.

QUESTION: HOW DO WE DETERMINE IDENTITY AND GENDER?

BIBLICAL WORLDVIEW EDUCATION ANSWER:	SECULARIZED WORLDVIEW EDUCATION ANSWER:
God created mankind in His own image; He created them male and female (Gen. 1:27). Gender is pre-determined by God and discoverable by the biological makeup of your body—either male or female.	Your biological sex and gender are not the same thing, and your gender is fluid and determined by how you feel about yourself at any given moment.

In a biblical worldview education, students are taught that identity and gender are created and defined by God. His design of two genders makes perfect sense in every way. God designed the male and female bodies to perfectly complement each other and created them to procreate. A man cannot create a baby with another man, nor can a woman create a baby with another woman. The vast majority of men and women are naturally attracted to the opposite sex. This is God's good design, and when kept within the bounds of marriage, it is absolutely one of the most beautiful parts of God's creation.

We also recognize that all of us are born with sin in our nature as a result of the fall and have greater or lesser tendencies toward yielding to different areas of the lust of the flesh. For some, the fall has produced a decline in genetics, which produces physical weaknesses like diabetes and heart disease, and we are not necessarily culpable for the diseases that might attack our fallen bodies. For others, things like a greater potential for alcoholism or a tendency toward some form of sexual deviancy might be a temptation that has been passed down through family genes.

My heart goes out to those who struggle with same-sex attraction and to the man or woman who is greatly tempted to be unfaithful to God and their spouse with a member of the opposite sex. In the rare occurrence that a person struggles with genuine gender dysphoria, I want to show deep compassion for that person. However, to tell a person who struggles with gender identity that they should just give in to those desires in order to become who they really are is no different than telling a married man to cheat on his wife if he feels like he wants to.

Young people must be taught the truth and convinced that aligning their lives with God's good design is the only path to happiness and His blessings. God's laws were put in place to protect us, not restrict us. God created us and knows exactly how we should live our lives. Telling Him we know better than He does is foolish and only produces the chaos we are seeing in our world today.

If a boy can declare out of the blue that he is a girl, why can't that same boy declare that he is a dog or a cat? As I mentioned earlier in this book, the "furries" reality is playing out in schools all across America. When we abandon God's good design, we become disconnected from reality, and the end result is insanity.

GOD'S GOOD DESIGN OF GENDER

There are only two genders/sexes: male and female. In the most basic sense, to be female means having a vagina, ovaries, XX chromosomes, predominant estrogen, and the ability to grow a baby in the abdominal area, and being male means having testes, a penis, XY chromosomes, predominant testosterone, and the ability to put a baby in a female's abdominal area by impregnating her egg with his sperm. Being biologically intersex can be any combination of these two.

According to the book *Mama Bear Apologetics Guide to Sexuality: Empowering Your Kids to Understand and Live Out God's Design*, a small but significant percentage of the population is born with sexual abnormalities (intersex) that make it a bit more difficult to determine one's gender.[1] We want to be compassionate in these cases and recognize that this can be very complex. However, even in these cases, which are brought about because of genetic abnormalities, there is never a third gender created. The Intersex Society of North America made this statement: "We are trying to make the world a safe place for intersex kids; we don't think labeling them with a third gender category that doesn't exist would help them."[2]

In *Mama Bear Apologetics Guide to Sexuality*, Hillary Ferrer expands on this definition of male and female by saying, "Being female doesn't necessarily mean that you have certain body parts. There are plenty of women who have either had hysterectomies or cancer, which required the removal of the uterus and ovaries, and they are no less female than a woman with ovaries and uterus. If I were to tweak this statement to be more accurate, I'd say that a woman is a person who possesses the genetic programming for these characteristics, which will be manifested unless abnormalities or tampering occur."[3] I would add here that this is also true about a male.

When an atheist expressed his surprise and embarrassment that only 35% of atheists in a poll thought minors should not be allowed to undergo gender transition procedures, conservative Christian commentator Allie Beth Stuckey gave an insightful response. She said, "Because science is an insufficient guide. Science only answers what is possible, not what's moral. It answers the question of can, but not the question of should. Science can tell us the biology of sex, but it cannot tell us why someone's feelings shouldn't trump their biological reality. The innocence of children, the sacredness of the body, etc., are theological, moral concepts not scientific ones."[4]

When children are taught in a secularized worldview education to view the world through a lens that removes God from the picture, confusion and chaos are the result. Across America, there has been a massive increase in gender identity issues, and there is one primary reason for this. Pop culture and educational leaders are leading our children to believe these awful lies. I will go so far as to say that I believe this will go down in history as one of the worst cases of child abuse ever known to mankind. The dismembering of young people's bodies through hormone treatment and surgeries is pure evil, and you don't want your child anywhere near people who might convince them to believe these lies.

The devil and the world he controls are playing for keeps. We must be extremely wise about who we allow to influence our children's lives. Our children must be taught the truth about who God is and who they are to guard them against the lies of the world so that they can experience the peace that is missing in the lives of so many of our youth today.

CHAPTER 17

How Do We Define the Family?

"A good father is one of the most unsung, unpraised, unnoticed, and yet one of the most valuable assets in our society."

Billy Graham

God defined the family as one man and one woman joined together in marriage, raising godly offspring. A biblical family is multigenerational and includes grandparents and extended family. We read about God's good design for the family in Gen. 2:18, 21-25.

> "Then the Lord God said, 'It is not good that the man should be alone; I will make him a helper fit for him.' . . . So the Lord God caused a deep sleep to fall upon the man, and while he slept took one of his ribs and closed up its place with flesh. And the rib that the Lord God had taken from the man he made into a woman and brought her to the man. Then the man said, 'This

at last is bone of my bones and flesh of my flesh; she shall be called Woman, because she was taken out of Man.' Therefore a man shall leave his father and his mother and hold fast to his wife, and they shall become one flesh. And the man and his wife were both naked and were not ashamed.'"

QUESTION: HOW DO WE DEFINE THE FAMILY?

BIBLICAL WORLDVIEW EDUCATION ANSWER:	SECULARIZED WORLDVIEW EDUCATION ANSWER:
God perfectly designed men and women to come together in marriage and raise godly offspring, and this arrangement works best in creating healthy children, families, and societies.	A family consists of the people you currently love or have feelings for and can include same-sex and multiple partners. There is no set arrangement for the people who form a family.

God's good design works out best in the real world, and research has overwhelmingly shown that the healthiest, happiest children grow up in a home with their mom and dad together.[1] We are watching chaos break loose on children in the world today because we are violating God's good design for the family. The attack on the family is straight out of hell, and it has happened in a thousand different ways. I am fully convinced that even Christian families have bought into the lies of our culture. If our children do not fully understand God's good design for the family, we are relegating them to a tragic future.

THE IMPORTANCE OF FATHERS

For example, God makes very clear in His Word how important fathers are to their children. Many in our world today denigrate men and fatherhood and even go so far as to say fathers are unnecessary in raising healthy children. It is estimated that almost twenty-five million children live absent from their biological fathers.[2] A full 43% of U.S. children are now living without their fathers.[3] The destruction of the family is at the core of the destruction of our nation, and research shows the devastation that takes place when children grow up without a father.[4] As shown in the following statistics gathered by The National Center for Fathering, the impact of fatherlessness on our nation is widespread.[5]

- 63% of youth suicides are from fatherless homes.
- 85% of youths in prisons grew up in a fatherless home.
- 80% of rapists with anger problems come from fatherless homes.
- 71% of high school dropouts come from fatherless homes.
- 85% of children who show behavior disorders come from fatherless homes.
- 90% of homeless and runaway children are from fatherless homes.
- 75% of adolescent patients in chemical abuse centers come from fatherless homes.
- 71% of pregnant teenagers lack a father.

Here's what commentator Rob Wood said on X about these statistics and fatherhood.

"This is just the tip of the iceberg. Tens of millions of children live in dad-deprived homes. Millions more have dads physically present, but emotionally absent. This is a national emergency. The stats are staggering. It is a real pandemic. Yet, with the mountains of data pouring in, many influential people controlling the cultural narrative STILL argue that fathers are simply not important. It is utterly demented and evil. Fatherlessness is associated with almost every societal ill facing our sons and daughters.

Involved fathers build strong families by default and enrich the communities around them. When fathers are involved the outcomes are TREMENDOUS across the board for children: Academic, social, physical, emotional, and mental health...nearly every category measured improves exponentially.

Children need good fathers. Families need good fathers. Communities need good fathers. Cities need good fathers. States need good fathers. Countries need good fathers. Let's abandon society's proclivity for shame, embarrassment, hatred and guilt toward boys and men. It isn't helpful. It's destructive. It's evil.

This is our most urgent social problem. We must re-create fatherhood as a VITAL social role for MEN. Reform is pointless if fatherhood isn't at the top of the list. This is the key to stopping the spread of male violence, rape, and anger. This is the key to closing down prisons. This is the key to closing the gap on poverty. This is the key to destroying the porn industry. This is the key to school achievement for struggling boys and girls. This is the key to greatly diminishing drug abuse. This is the key to eradicating youth suicide. This is the key to stamping out bullying and violent crime.

We can't depend on the government (and shouldn't). We can't depend on Hollywood. We can't depend on advertisers. We must work together in our families, communities and neighborhoods to forge a new path forward and to build a better future.[6]

I couldn't agree more with Rob! Here's the thing that ought to awaken parents like nothing else. Secularized education today is in all-out attack mode against the family. Our children who are enrolled in secularized schools, be they private or public, are being misled, and the end result is that many children from Christian homes are not embracing God's good design for the family. Because of this, they do not understand God's plan for the roles of men and women, husbands and wives, parents and children, and grandparents and grandchildren. A Christian education, given through the family, church, and school, ensures that God's ideas become the core belief of our children in this area and so many others.

CHAPTER 18

What Is Wrong With This World?

"Education without values, as useful as it is, seems rather to make man a more clever devil."

C.S. Lewis

Why is there so much evil in this world? All of humanity is asking this question, and every worldview is desperately trying to answer it. How we view God will ultimately determine how we answer this question and whether or not we arrive at the right solutions to help us conquer the evil in our world.

QUESTION: WHAT IS WRONG WITH THIS WORLD?

BIBLICAL WORLDVIEW EDUCATION ANSWER:	SECULARIZED WORLDVIEW EDUCATION ANSWER:
Men and women brought the curse of sin into this world when they chose to rebel against the holy God who created us, and therefore, all humans are born with sin in their nature and are bent on doing evil (Gen. 3).	Humans are highly evolved animals driven by our chemical makeup and instincts and are basically good. We do bad things when we are corrupted by the surrounding environment.

The ultimate worldview question of why there is so much evil in this world has been used by Satan to drive more people away from God than perhaps any other argument. I remember an interesting conversation I had with an atheist on a flight. As I boarded the plane and sat down, the gentleman beside me asked where I was coming from and why I had been in town. I mentioned I had given a speech the night before, and he asked, "What kind of speech?" When I told him I gave a speech on biblical worldview, he quickly mentioned he was raised Southern Baptist but had abandoned the faith decades ago and was now an atheist. He said he had abandoned the faith because he never could understand how a good God could allow so much evil in the world.

I responded, "Since you don't believe God exists, let's just assume that He doesn't for the sake of this conversation." I then said, "Now you tell me why so much evil exists." I continued by asking him if he was a Darwinian evolutionist, and he said,

"Yes." I asked him if he believed humans were evolving and getting better and better, and again, he said, "Yes." I then looked at him and asked, "Are we really getting better and better?" He responded, "Actually, I think we're getting worse." We had a wonderful conversation, and as we were about to get off the plane, he asked me for my card and said, "I may want to talk to you some more."

My point in sharing this story is to say that all worldviews have to answer for the existence of evil, and I am convinced the biblical worldview answer makes the most sense in explaining evil and gives the most hope for a solution. A secularized worldview has no basis even to declare what is good or bad, much less explain why evil exists, and it certainly doesn't have a good solution. Only the biblical worldview explains our actions, holds us accountable, and provides a way for mankind to be redeemed from the power of evil.

THE MISDIAGNOSIS OF EVIL

We all know you can only fix a problem once you correctly identify it. When the problem of evil is misdiagnosed in an educational setting, our children suffer. The consequences of not teaching children the truth about the problem of evil reverberate throughout their entire lives as they try to fix something that has never been properly diagnosed.

What a school teaches about the problem of evil in our world plays a significant role in a child's success or failure. The educational methodologies employed in most secularized schools do not understand human nature or account for sin and rebellion in a child's heart. These teaching methods allow children to operate without restraint and with little direction and fail to help them reach their full potential. They may mean well, but children left to themselves will become little monsters, and once they reach adulthood, they will be unable to succeed in the real world.

Children must be taught the truth of the Bible so they can apply it to their lives. Billy Graham once was asked, "If Christianity is valid, why is there so much evil in the world?" He replied, "With so much soap, why are there so many dirty people in the world? Christianity, like soap, must be personally applied if it is to make a difference in our lives." A biblical worldview education will teach our children the truth about the world and who they are so that they can become all God has created them to be.

CHAPTER 19

How Do We Fix What Is Broken In This World?

"In the midst of an ever-changing world, the good news is that the life of faith is anchored by the power, provisions, and promises of God. Circumstances may change, but the future is as sure as the character of God Himself. No matter what happens, those who trust in God hope in His word."

Scott Hafemann

There are many different theories among those who reject a biblical worldview regarding how we should fix our broken world. The following secularized worldview answer is perhaps the most common layman's understanding of what our children are being taught in non-Christian educational settings.

QUESTION: HOW DO WE FIX IS BROKEN IN THIS WORLD?

BIBLICAL WORLDVIEW EDUCATION ANSWER:	SECULARIZED WORLDVIEW EDUCATION ANSWER:
Jesus Christ redeems us from sin by securing our redemption through His physical death, burial, and resurrection. Through repentance and faith, the Holy Spirit regenerates, indwells, and empowers us to become agents of redemption and restoration.	We must continuously evolve, develop our scientific understanding of every field, and advance technology until we conquer all natural things that bring sickness and evil into the world.

Modernism is the idea that technology and science hold all the answers to the world's problems, and postmodernism is the idea that we can't really know truth. Even though modernism has been philosophically rejected as a whole and replaced by postmodernism, there is still a pervasive belief that science and technology are the keys to fixing the problems of mankind.

As discussed in the last chapter, you cannot fix the problem if you don't diagnose it correctly. In most non-Christian school settings, children are taught insufficient solutions because a secularized worldview cannot accurately diagnose the problem. Secularized education disregards the biblical idea that all of us are born with sin in our nature and are bent to do wrong. When education refuses to accept God's thinking about how to fix the problem, they will continually propose solutions that lead our children further astray.

For example, when God designed sex, He created it to be

enjoyed inside the marriage union with the primary purpose that it would produce godly offspring. Because of sin, people want to engage in sex outside of God's plan. Secularized education teaches children they are highly evolved animals and their sex drive should not be repressed. Some psychologists have foolishly claimed that repression of the sex drive will damage a child, and therefore, we should let children explore sexual desires.

Lest you think this type of perversion isn't being taught in the mainstream, read what The National Sexual Violence Resource Center (NSVRC) recommends as behavior falling within healthy childhood sexual development: "Children are being playful and/or curious, not aggressive or angry," and "play involving sexuality (i.e. playing Doctor, 'Show me yours/I'll show you mine') should be with a child of a similar age and developmental level, not with a much older or younger child."[1] This publication, titled "An Overview of Healthy Childhood Sexual Development," was posted on the website of The National Children's Advocacy Center (NCAC). These national agencies advocate that healthy childhood sexual development should exhibit sexual behaviors so long as they're playful and curious and with a child of similar age and developmental level!

DIRE CONSEQUENCES FOR FALSE SOLUTIONS

Teaching children unbiblical views of sex has dire implications in the real world. An attorney from California told me that 50% of all teens in the Los Angeles area have a sexually transmitted disease. When children are encouraged to embrace immorality and are not taught to address sex outside of marriage as a sin, they deal with the ill effects of the sexual revolution that is destroying their lives.

We have seen the impact of misdiagnosing the root cause of crime in our cities. Prosecutors who have been miseducated to believe poverty and racism are the root causes of crime believe the system has oppressed these people and that they should not be held responsible for their actions. Therefore, when criminals are arrested, these prosecutors refuse to prosecute most crimes, and criminals are often quickly released back onto the streets. Again, they do not understand the problem of sin in a person's heart and the fact that God holds every human accountable for their actions. In the name of social justice, they have abandoned true justice, and it is destroying our major cities.

Children who spend over 16,000 hours in a school that never teaches them the true solutions to the world's problems will not be well-equipped to succeed. In a biblical worldview educational setting, children are taught God's view of sin and right and wrong and that every human will stand before God someday and be held accountable for their actions. When children realize how hard it is to obey God's laws, we introduce them to Jesus, the One who can do such mighty work in their hearts that they develop a love for what is right. They learn Christ came to redeem humans from sin and all the brokenness it produces, and the physical death, burial, and resurrection of Jesus secured this redemption. When we repent of our sins and trust Him to save us, we are regenerated and indwelt by His Spirit and become empowered to know His will and follow His plans. As we do this, we become agents of redemption and restoration in every sphere of our world. The saving work of Jesus and the implementation of His will on earth is the cure for all that is wrong in this world.

CHAPTER 20

How Do We Define Morality?

"It is impossible to have a divinely sanctioned morality if God is not the object of and motive for it."

John Hannah

No doubt you have heard someone say, "Well, that may be your truth, but it's not my truth." This understanding of truth is rooted in the postmodern idea that there is no universal, absolute standard of right and wrong that applies to all humans at all times. This is the fundamental principle that dominates all forms of secularized education in America.

QUESTION: HOW DO WE DEFINE MORALITY?

BIBLICAL WORLDVIEW EDUCATION ANSWER:	SECULARIZED WORLDVIEW EDUCATION ANSWER:
God gave us a moral code out of His holy nature that helps humans and the world thrive and function in a way that produces peace, productivity, and prosperity.	There is no absolute moral code. Humans define morality as they choose and as it is useful for the survival of the species.

I'm not saying that secularized educational systems aren't teaching a moral code. Actually, they are extremely dogmatic about their moral code. If you think I'm exaggerating, look up all the people in schools who have gotten into trouble for using the wrong pronouns when speaking to a transgender person. What's so interesting to me is that the same people who teach there is no absolute standard of right and wrong are some of the most intolerant and dogmatic people about what they believe to be right and wrong.

One of the strongest pieces of evidence that there is a God and that humans have His image stamped upon them is the universal idea of right and wrong that has been found in every people group on earth. I know of missionaries who wandered into villages filled with cannibals and yet discovered they were afraid of the God up above. They had a moral code they tried to follow, even though it took an introduction to Jesus and the Word of God to deliver these tribes from cannibalism. Many people today idolize primitive Indian tribes as if they somehow were living these beautiful, peaceful lives until Christians showed up. This idea couldn't be further from the truth. All of these primitive groups of people practiced evil, including things like human sacrifice, slavery, and massive sexual abuse. History testifies that those who align their lives and societies with God's moral standard are the most secure, productive, and safe societies on earth. This is true because God created the universe and designed how everything should operate in accordance with what is true, good, and beautiful.

Christian morality across the centuries liberated enslaved people and women en masse, created the first hospitals and universities, and brought more compassion and charity to the world than any other worldview or core set of beliefs. In his book *What If Jesus Had Never Been Born* D. James Kennedy said, "Despite its humble origins, the Church has made more changes on earth for the good than any other movement or force in history."[1] Why? Because Christianity is true, good, and beautiful.

The United States of America and a small number of other countries that were shaped by Christian thought happen to be the places on earth where millions of people are still desperately trying to get into. You will never hear of a mass migration into Russia, China, or North Korea. As American education stripped God's truth from its curricula, it has failed to teach children the beauty of the biblical worldview. As a result, we are moving further and further away from the ideals that created our nation as the most powerful and prosperous nation in world history. Half of America now believes Christianity is something to be shunned and ridiculed. If we are not able to raise up a new generation of Christian thinkers and leaders, we are headed for the total cultural breakdown of our nation.

THE DEVASTATING IMPACT OF FALSE WORLDVIEWS

Cultural Marxism has already taken deep root in the minds of millions of Americans, and those who embrace this false worldview are bent on destroying our current systems and rebuilding America on Marxist values and principles. In case you're not familiar with the term Marxism, in its simplest form, it is the idea that in every society, there is a group of oppressors and a group that is oppressed. The goal of Marxism in its many iterations is to see the oppressed overthrow the oppressors and implement equity in the so-called name of fairness and equality for all. In economic Marxism, the state controls all private property, industry, media, banking, and more. In theory, the state redistributes wealth so all workers have what they need to live a healthy and happy life. However, everywhere Marxism has been implemented, it has turned the state into a totalitarian tyrant, with a few rich and powerful people dominating the vast majority of citizens who are unbelievably poor. Since individuals don't own property or businesses, their incentive is destroyed and despair dominates.

For example, Ukraine had been dominated by Soviet Communist Marxism for decades when my sister went there as a missionary after Communist Marxism collapsed in the Soviet Union. In the middle of one afternoon, Sandy took her large family to a downtown, government-owned pizza shop in Kyiv. The man running the restaurant was standing outside, and even though they had arrived during the hours when the pizza shop was open, the man refused to serve them. He simply didn't feel like making any more pizzas. In that system, it didn't matter if he sold one pizza or one hundred pizzas because he would make the same amount of money either way.

American secularized education glorifies many false

worldviews and refuses to teach the truth about the Christian worldview and moral code. This is having a devastating impact on our young people. A few years ago, a very successful businessman told me, "I'm not sure if I will be able to keep my company open in ten years." When I asked him why, he said, "I can't find an eighteen-year-old with a good attitude."

Out of God's holy nature, He has given us a moral code that helps humans thrive and the world function in a way that produces peace, productivity, and prosperity, and when we fully surrender to and embrace God's good design and follow His plan, humans flourish. When we abandon His plan, chaos naturally follows. When we teach children the truth about God and His expectations for all of life, we set them up for success. This is no trivial matter, and as parents, we must ensure our children are taught God's truth all day, every day.

Thank you for taking the time to take a deeper dive into the issue of education. In the next section of the book, I want to offer a direct challenge to parents.

SECTION 4

Five Reasons Noah Was Able to Save His Family In a World Gone Crazy

CHAPTER 21

A Man God Used to Save Humanity and His Family

*"And God blessed Noah and his sons and said to them,
'Be fruitful and multiply and fill the earth.'"*

Genesis 9:1

Noah was a man God used to save humanity from extinction but also to save his own family. Please take the time to read the account of his life with fresh eyes, and then let's think together about some things that were key in Noah saving his family from destruction.

The Lord saw that the wickedness of man was great in the earth, and that every intention of the thoughts of his heart was only evil continually. And the Lord regretted that he had made man on the earth, and it grieved him to his heart. So the Lord said, "I will blot out man whom I have created from the face of the land, man and animals and creeping things and birds of the heavens, for I am sorry that I have made them." But Noah found favor in the eyes of the Lord.

Noah and the Flood

These are the generations of Noah. Noah was a righteous man, blameless in his generation. Noah walked with God. And Noah had three sons, Shem, Ham, and Japheth. Now the earth was corrupt in God's sight, and the earth was filled with violence. And God saw the earth, and behold, it was corrupt, for all flesh had corrupted their way on the earth. And God said to Noah, "I have determined to make an end of all flesh, for the earth is filled with violence through them. Behold, I will destroy them with the earth. Make yourself an ark of gopher wood. Make rooms in the ark, and cover it inside and out with pitch. This is how you are to make it: the length of the ark 300 cubits, its breadth 50 cubits, and its height 30 cubits. Make a roof for the ark, and finish it to a cubit above, and set the door of the ark in its side. Make it with lower, second, and third decks. For behold, I will bring a flood of waters upon the earth to destroy all flesh in which is the breath of life under heaven. Everything that is on the earth shall die. But I will establish my covenant with you, and you shall come into the ark, you, your sons, your wife, and your sons' wives with you. And of every living thing of all flesh, you shall bring two of every sort into the ark to keep them alive with you. They shall be male and female. Of the birds according to their kinds, and of the animals according to their kinds, of every creeping thing of the ground, according to its kind, two of every sort shall come in to you to keep them alive. Also take with you every sort of food that is eaten, and store it up. It shall serve as food for you and for them." Noah did this; he did all that God commanded him (Gen. 6:5-22).

Noah was six hundred years old when the flood of waters came upon the earth. And Noah and his sons and his wife and his sons' wives with him went into the ark to escape the waters of the flood (Gen. 7:6-7).

By faith Noah, being warned by God concerning events as yet unseen, in reverent fear constructed an ark for the saving of his household. By this he condemned the world and became an heir of the righteousness that comes by faith (Heb. 11:7).

I find it intriguing that the writer of Hebrews defines Noah's reason for building an ark as "the saving of his household." We all know the biblical account of Noah's Ark and the great worldwide flood. Although God was saving mankind from extinction, the writer of Hebrews emphasizes Noah's deep motivation to save his own household.

Noah is mentioned on several occasions in the New Testament. In Matthew 24, the disciples asked Jesus, "What will be the sign of your coming and of the end of the age?" Jesus gave a lengthy answer, and as part of that answer, He gave us these words:

"But concerning that day and hour no one knows, not even the angels of heaven, nor the Son, but the

Father only. For as were the days of Noah, so will be the coming of the Son of Man. For as in those days before the flood they were eating and drinking, marrying and giving in marriage, until the day when Noah entered the ark, and they were unaware until the flood came and swept them all away, so will be the coming of the Son of Man" (Matt. 24:36-39).

Earlier, we read about the days of Noah in Genesis: "The Lord saw that the wickedness of man was great in the earth, and that every intention of the thoughts of his heart was only evil continually" (v. 5) and "Now the earth was corrupt in God's sight, and the earth was filled with violence" (v. 11). I don't think I have to convince you that we are living in the days of Noah once again.

OUR WORLD TODAY

A few years ago, people didn't seem to grasp the importance of RenewaNation's mission to give millions of children a biblical worldview. That's not so much the case today. Our impact and reach are growing by leaps and bounds because parents and grandparents have been awakened to the fact that Satan and the world are aggressively coming after our children. We truly live in a world gone crazy.

I sometimes wonder what God thinks and says as He looks at our world today. The major difference between our world and Noah's is that there are millions of genuine Noahs— Christ-followers who have been redeemed by His blood and are walking with Him in faith and obedience. We have huge advantages over Noah in spite of the godless world we live in today. We have been given the enabling power and presence of the Holy Spirit and the totality of the Bible to instruct, guide, and encourage us to do what God has called us to do.

Even though our world is exceedingly wicked and headed for judgment, millions of dads and moms, like Noah, are fighting to save their families. I have no doubt that most of you reading this book fit into this group. If God could help Noah save his family in a world where he was the only righteous man and had to build a massive ship to save them, He can help us save our children and grandchildren. And that's great news!

CHAPTER 22

Noah Was a Man Who Was Right With God

"No one can sum up all God is able to accomplish through one solitary life, wholly yielded, adjusted, and obedient to Him."

D.L. Moody

Over the coming chapters, let's examine five reasons Noah was able to save his family in a world gone crazy. The first reason was that *he was a man who was right with God.* Genesis 6:8-9 says, "Noah found favor in the eyes of the Lord," and "Noah was a righteous man, blameless in his generation. Noah walked with God." In Genesis 7:1, the Lord said to Noah, "Go into the ark, you and all your household, for I have seen that you are righteous before me in this generation."

The most important thing in saving our families is for us as parents and grandparents to be in a deep and authentic relationship with Jesus Christ. Parents who do not serve Christ are the number one obstacle to seeing children serve Christ.

There never has been, nor ever will be, a mom or dad who lives a perfect Christian life. However, if we hope for our children to be saved from Satan's destructive plans for their lives, we must, as parents, have an authentic relationship with Christ that fills us with humility and transparency in our homes.

One of the main reasons that almost all of the nearly 170 Keatons who are of age in my family are walking with Christ today is that we had a dad and mom who authentically walked with Christ behind the scenes. We saw them on platforms across this country, but how we saw them live off the platform was more important by far. I remember looking through the keyhole of my mom's bedroom door and seeing her on her knees in prayer, weeping over our souls and the burdens of her life.

I'll never forget the day our dad came home from a busy preaching trip and lost his cool because we had not followed his instructions while he was away. I had never seen my dad so angry and loud, and we scattered to the four corners of our house and property. I remember his anger that day, but what I remember most is him gathering us all in the living room and weeping as he asked for our forgiveness. Pure joy replaced deep disappointment as I saw my dad take responsibility for his failure.

Kids aren't looking for perfection; they are looking for authenticity and to see that Jesus is real in the hardest moments of life. In all my years of ministry, the most difficult young person to reach with the gospel has been that young person whose parents failed to live authentic Christian lives in their home. I've watched young people sit in excellent apologetic classes and experience services where God's convincing and convicting presence was powerfully manifested, but many of them just didn't seem to get it. I've now concluded, after over thirty years of full-time ministry, that the most common link among the precious young people who refused to embrace Christianity was parents who were hypocritical or inauthentic in some way in their relationship with Jesus.

I was talking with one of my nieces, who was in her early thirties at the time of our discussion, and she said something that shocked me. This niece had grown up in our Christian school and one of our church plants. She told me seven young people her age who had grown up in our ministry were already divorced. I asked her to name them, and as she did, I immediately identified that in six of the seven cases, one or more of the parents in their lives were not authentic followers of Christ. Placing our children in great churches and schools will go a long way toward helping them become followers of Christ, but the most critical factor is how their parents live at home.

THE IMPACT OF BROKEN RELATIONSHIPS

Let me add here: Divorce is a bomb that will leave a crater in your child's life that, in some ways, will last a lifetime. It should be avoided if at all possible. If you've already been through a divorce, I don't want you to feel as if there's no hope for your children. There is much hope, but they will have more to overcome. God will help your children just like He helped my wife.

Divorce is sometimes unavoidable and allowed by Scripture. Perhaps you have experienced this. God cares deeply for you and your children, and He has special grace for your family. Some of you may live with deep regret over personal failures that broke up your family. If you are truly repentant, Christ will forgive you and restore much of the brokenness in your life and family.

If you're still married to the father or mother of your children, do whatever it takes to stay together for life. Yes, almost any marriage can be renewed and repaired. I have seen the worst situations you can imagine restored. Find a biblical pastor or counselor and re-surrender your will to God's way. He will work miracles that your children will benefit from forever.

AN HONEST QUESTION

Dad and Mom, let me ask you a question. If you were to be totally honest with yourself and God today, could you say that you are walking in an intimate, obedient relationship with Jesus? Maybe you have never fully surrendered your life to Christ by repenting of your sins (Acts 3:19) and placing all your hope for salvation in Him alone (Acts 16:31). Maybe you've never been brought from spiritual death to spiritual life (Eph. 2:1-5) by being born again (John 3:1-3). If this is your situation, Christ took your sin upon Himself and experienced the full wrath of a holy and just God so that you can be forgiven for every sin you have ever committed. With the help of God's Spirit that dwells in every true Christian, you can live an authentic Christian life in your home and in front of your children. This is the best way to ensure your children will be saved for all eternity. Right now, I encourage and invite you to confess your sins and place all of your trust in Jesus to forgive you and give you a new spiritual life. Don't rush past this! Are you ready to trust in Christ alone to save you? Seek His forgiveness right now, throw yourself at His feet, and He will save you. If you have trusted Christ for salvation as a result of reading this, please contact us at info@renewanation.org to receive an additional resource to help you in your new walk with Christ.

Maybe you are a parent who knows you have been born again, but you have allowed Satan to misalign your priorities, or you have grown cold in your love for the Lord. You have lately failed to make raising godly children one of the highest priorities of your life. Right now, I encourage you to repent before the Lord and gather your family for a meeting where you will apologize and get things back on track. This can be hard because perhaps you've allowed your children to get involved in things you must now move them away from. Perhaps you have stopped practicing habits like regular church attendance and family devotions. It will take courage and conviction to get things moving again in the right direction, but your children will someday thank you. They will likely resist and fuss about it now, but later they will recognize that you did what was best for them. Dads and Moms, fall in love with Jesus, live authentically at home, and Jesus will help you save your children!

CHAPTER 23

Noah Believed What God Said

"That's what it means to live by faith—God reveals Himself to us, and we respond to Him trustingly, taking Him at His Word."

Iain Duguid

The second reason Noah was able to save his family was that *he believed what God said.* God told Noah to build an enormous ship on dry ground because He was going to send a massive flood to destroy the world. "Make yourself an ark of gopher wood. Make rooms in the ark, and cover it inside and out with pitch" (Gen. 6:14). It sounded crazy! If you want to see a lifesize replica of this ship, visit the Ark Encounter in Williamstown, Kentucky. This massive ship is 510 feet long, eighty-five feet wide, and fifty-one feet high!

Noah was the only man in the world who believed what God said. No doubt, millions of people thought Noah had lost his mind when he built the ark, but because Noah believed God and was obedient to God's commands, he saved his family from the flood. If we're going to save our families in a world gone crazy, we have to get back to ordering our lives by the truth of God's Word, not the falsehood and peer pressure that dominates our culture.

For all of human history, Satan has been following the same deceptive game plan when trying to lead people to disbelieve what God has said. In Genesis 3:1, the first question Satan posed to Eve in the Garden of Eden was, "Did God really say?" He immediately followed that question by calling God a liar when he stated, "You shall not surely die if you eat of the fruit of this tree" (v. 4). Satan then took his scheme one step further by accusing God of wanting to prevent humans from reaching their full potential when he said, "For God knows that when you eat of it your eyes will be opened, and you will be like God, knowing good and evil" (v. 5).

Too many Christian parents are getting their marching orders from this world rather than from God's Word. Many of the so-called Christian parenting books in publication today are not based deeply on the Bible. They are a superficial mixture of pop psychology, tradition, and current parenting trends. The only guidebook that will never change is God's Word.

RESPECT FOR GOD'S AUTHORITY

Let me give you just one example of what I'm talking about. One of the most foundational principles in the Bible concerning how we are to raise our children is respect for God and all God-ordained authority structures. In *50 Things Every Child Needs to Know Before Leaving Home*, a book written by Dr. Josh Mulvihill and published by RenewaNation, Dr. Mulvihill lists respecting God-ordained authority as the first principle important for children to understand. God's Word instructs parents to teach and discipline children so they will learn the fear of the Lord and to respect and obey their parents (Eph. 6:1; Prov. 19:18; Heb. 12:9-10). Child psychologists, untethered from biblical truth, have eroded God's teaching in this area, and the end result has been disastrous. As always, children suffer the most when we ignore God's design.

All parents have likely had a child embarrass them in public, but a child who is not intentionally taught to respect and obey authority is a child who will not have a successful life. I was eating in a restaurant and sitting close to a young couple with a little boy who looked to be about three years old. He was throwing a fit, and the parents kept trying to bribe him to get him to behave. They told him that if he behaved, they would buy him something at the store when they left the restaurant. He never stopped acting out and ruined everyone's meal around him. This child had parents who had been taught principles of child-rearing that do not work and damage children's lives. This child would have a much brighter future if his parents believed and followed God's Word.

One thing I often hear from my teacher friends who teach in public schools, and even some in Christian schools, is that children today are out of control. Many teachers are walking away from public education because serious discipline is no longer allowed in many schools. One teacher told me about a student who broke out a window, threw his desk across the room, and was never even seriously disciplined. This precious female teacher was scared for her life every day at school.

Satan is the father of rebellion, and he has led our world today to normalize rebellion. Look at our inner cities, where prosecutors refuse to charge people for serious crimes. Even leaders in our nation fail to hold people accountable for entering our nation illegally. When we don't believe God's Word in any area of life, chaos will follow.

BOLDLY STANDING FOR CHRIST

Satan and the world he controls give Christian parents a thousand false ideas about how to raise their children. The world will tell you it's normal for your child to watch, listen to, and be involved in all kinds of stuff that is destructive according to God's Word. When most other Christian families allow their children to look like the world, talk like the world, and take part in sinful and lustful things in the world, it can be difficult to take a stand, especially when your children are begging you to be like everyone else. Can you imagine the pressure Noah's kids faced as their dad built a massive boat while telling people a great flood was coming to destroy the earth? I have often wondered how hard it was for Noah to convince his children to get on the ark and shut the door.

I praise God for my dad, who saw what was coming and made bold moves to save us children long before it was popular. He launched a Christian school in 1976 because of what he saw happening, even then, in public schools. I recently asked my nearly eighty-year-old father what gave him the impetus to start a Christian school when there were so few Christian schools. Dad recounted several attacks on the Christian faith which he had to fight against in the public schools in those days. I have no doubt his willingness to believe God's Word and stand against the prevailing Christian culture is one reason that over ninety members of his direct descendants are in vocational Christian ministry or preparing to go into ministry.

I tried my best to believe and obey God's Word, no matter what others were doing when we were raising our daughters. Occasionally, they would say, "Dad, why can't we do that? Other kids in the church are allowed to." I told them I wasn't responsible for what other people allowed their children to do, but I was fully responsible for what I allowed them to do because I would stand before God one day and give an account of how I had stewarded their lives.

Dads and Moms, you must stop caring about what neighbors or fellow church members are thinking and doing and start caring about what God's Word tells you to do. Sometimes, to save your children, you must separate them or yourself from influences and people working against what God has to say. Noah believed what God was saying, and eventually Noah walked into the ark with his family, and God shut them in. It was the only way Noah could save his children.

Good things happen when we believe what God says is true and follow His good design. In order to believe and obey God's Word, we must know God's Word. Parents, I encourage you to read the Bible from beginning to end each year. Yes, I know certain books in the Bible are more enjoyable than others, but reading God's Word regularly shapes our thinking and behavior in profound ways. I have learned that before something can become a joy, it must first become a discipline, and the discipline of reading God's Word has become an irreplaceable delight in my life. I have used a simple Bible reading plan for many years to stay on track. Receive a copy of this plan by contacting info@renewanation.org. Reading the entire Bible in a year only takes fifteen minutes a day. If we, as dads and moms, trust God's Word and live according to His plan, we can save our families just as Noah did.

CHAPTER 24

Noah Understood and Faithfully Followed God's Plan for His Family

"Much of the confusion that characterizes our society is the result of the violation of God's design. The blueprint has been lost."

Elisabeth Elliot

Noah saved his family because *he understood and faithfully followed God's plan for his family*. In his case, it involved making considerable changes to his lifestyle and priorities, and he had to spend decades physically building an ark of protection. He had to set everything else aside and stay focused on this one primary mission.

If we're going to save our children, we, too, must get reacquainted with God's plan for the family and be willing to take all the necessary steps to follow His plan, which has been given to us in His Word. Let's briefly explore God's plan for the family while understanding that exceptional circumstances and callings sometimes prevent people from experiencing every aspect of God's plan. In those situations, God brings special grace, favor, and purpose.

GOD'S DESIGN FOR THE FAMILY AND PURPOSE FOR PARENTING

God designed men and women to come together in marriage at a fairly young age and stay together for a lifetime. He has given husbands and wives equal value but unique roles that produce harmony in marriage and society when embraced (Eph. 5:22-33). God calls husbands to provide for, protect, and lead the family, while wives are called to come alongside their husbands as they bear children, nurture the family, and make their home a haven. This arrangement can look very different from family to family, but when God-given roles are not honored, families struggle to be successful.

Far too many Christian families have embraced a model of the family that is unbiblical and unproductive for raising godly children, and it has had a devastating impact on our entire society. I believe one of the main reasons so many children are insecure, struggle emotionally, and are overly influenced by their peers and society at large is that they have not had the proper amount of time with their parents, especially time focused on true discipleship.

In Deuteronomy 6:4-9, we are commanded as parents to diligently teach our children God's truth ". . . when you sit in your house, and when you walk by the way, and when you lie down, and when you rise" (v. 7). All day, every day, we are to be pouring God's truth into the hearts and minds of our children. This parenting journey isn't just a small part of God's plan; it is central to His plan to spread the gospel and disciple the next generation. This is why those who intentionally reject having children are violating an essential piece of God's plan for humanity.

Let me say something that might raise some eyebrows, but I believe it is true. We've sold our souls to the American dream, where both parents are forced to spend more time at work than they do with their children. I realize we live in challenging financial times, and the entire economy is built on both parents working full-time. However, I challenge young families to take drastic measures so that at least one parent is home with the children as much as possible. Do whatever it takes to get out of debt and reduce your spending so that you can spend more time with your children and, as a result, become the number one influence in your children's lives.

In a majority of young families, it is necessary for both husband and wife to produce income. Many moms have learned to earn income from home, and if they have to work outside the home, they arrange for a close family member to watch their children. In our daughter Heidi's case, she is the children's ministry director at her church, and on the two weekdays when she is at the church, my wife is able to watch her children. This gives a great opportunity for their nana to pour into their young lives. In cases where a close family member is unavailable, arrange for someone who shares your values and whom you trust deeply to care for your children. Every family faces different circumstances, especially single parents, and God will pour grace into each family as needed, but the goal is for parents to be the primary influencers of their children.

EMBRACING A MORE BIBLICAL VISION
FOR WOMEN AND MOTHERHOOD

During World War II, mothers were forced to go to work to build weaponry for their husbands who were at war. Unfortunately, after the war ended, many American families raised their standard of living to match the salaries of two working parents. They adopted as a permanent practice what was meant to be a temporary solution during a time of crisis. According to *The Feminist Turned HouseWife on X (@antifemwife)*, "In 1910 almost 90% of women were home with their children. Now it's only 27% of women that stay home with their children."[1]

Radical feminists denigrated stay-at-home moms so much that it became unpopular to stay at home and raise children, and children have suffered the most. Feminists have accused women who choose to stay at home and raise their children of being enslaved to their husbands and children. However, those same women celebrate a woman who goes to work for fifty hours each week and works like a slave for a person who is not her husband and a company that likely couldn't care less about her. How is that freedom? Does it really make sense to work all week outside the home just to turn around and give a significant percentage of your pay to another person to watch your child?

Thankfully, there has been a strong backlash to feminism, especially since the COVID-19 pandemic. Significant voices are reminding us of the beauty and privilege of being a mother and wife. A growing number of young men and women are once again embracing a more biblical model of the family. They are getting married, having children, building a life with their spouse, and finding true meaning in life. They recognize that to be truly healthy, children need fathers and mothers who are highly active in their lives.

After reading what I have written, I am sure some of you are debating whether or not you should continue reading this book. Before you put it down, please think with me a little further. God gave women highly exceptional abilities to bear, nurture, and raise their children. No one on earth can care for a child like that child's mother. Women have been told that being the mother of a child is somehow inferior to having a distinguished career. Nothing could be further from the truth. I asked a new mother the other day if she had ever experienced anything like motherhood, and her face lit up as she said, "Nothing in this world compares." Ladies, don't let the lies this world has been telling you cheat you out of one of the most meaningful experiences a woman can ever have. And, just FYI, you can't imagine how awesome being a grandmother is. Just ask my wife!

If these ideas are new to you, I encourage you to join a community of women who have embraced a more biblical model of motherhood. A mother with many good things to offer on this subject is @BiblicalBeauty on X/Twitter. A couple of good books on this subject are *The Excellent Wife: A Biblical Perspective* by Martha Peace and *True Woman 101: Divine Design* by Mary A. Kassian and Nancy Leigh DeMoss.

Moms, the thankless hours you work to care for your children may go unnoticed at the moment, but you are building emotional strength deep within the hearts and minds of your children. Keep marching on—even when you are overwhelmed. You are doing exactly what you should do. I remember my mom sometimes crying while raising us nine children. I didn't like seeing her cry, but it didn't bother me too much because she never stopped meeting our needs. Mothers are generally more in touch with their children's feelings than fathers are because God designed women to be highly relational. Children need a mother's tender loving care, and those who do not have the nurturing care of a mother in their early years experience significant challenges.

CAPTURING A BIBLICAL VISION FOR MEN AND FATHERHOOD

Not only has motherhood and being a wife been attacked, but being a good husband and father have also been assaulted by the world around us. Men have been depicted in movies and pop culture as brutes who only want to drink beer, watch sports, and have sex. So many men have allowed themselves to live according to the lust of the flesh that women have stopped trusting them, and the thought of submitting oneself to a husband has become detestable. Men, what woman would want to allow us leadership in their lives if we can't be trusted to follow the scriptural command to love our wives like Christ loved the church?

Despite the failures of men, it is still God's good design that men lead their families and love their wives and children seriously and sacrificially. We are to serve our families and provide for them in every way possible. Our wives should never have to beg us to be responsible financially, spiritually, or in any other way. When men follow Christ and lead and love as He does, women find it a great joy to follow their husband's leadership. Earlier in this book, I made the case for the value of fathers in their children's lives. There simply is no substitute for a father in a child's life.

Dads, your influence and presence in your children's lives are so important. You are naturally the hero of your children.

You make them feel safe and protected. They will emulate you, whether for good or bad. If you take your relationship with God seriously, they likely will. If you make sports your god, they likely will. If you don't pay attention to your daughters, they will soon find other men who will. Men, let's embrace our role as leaders and guide and nurture our families according to God's design.

UNDERSTANDING GOD'S DESIGN FOR MARRIAGE AND SEXUALITY

Major research projects have shown that the happiest, healthiest, and longest-lasting marriages are those who marry young, do not cohabitate before marriage, and abstain from sex before marriage. A summary of a study conducted by the Institute for Family Studies (IFS) says, "Consistent with prior research, couples who cohabited before marriage were more likely to see their marriages end than those who did not cohabit before marriage."[2] Another study performed by IFS found that "premarital sex increases the chances of divorce between twofold and threefold."[3]

I must pause here and offer encouragement because perhaps you are thinking, "Oh my, what a failure I have been. I didn't follow God's plan in many ways. How can I ever help my children follow His plan?" I have great news for you. God is the God of grace and healing, and He knows how to redeem every one of our lives, no matter how much we have messed up. Don't spend too much time focusing on what you have done wrong in the past because our goal here is to help your children get it right in the present.

Your children will receive tremendous pressure from their friends to become sexually active at a young age and delay marriage and childbearing until much later in life. They will be challenged to "get their life together" before they get married, which often means financial stability, owning a home, and securing a great career. I am not recommending that young people get married without planning and evidence that both are responsible young adults. However, it is much easier to build wealth when two young people get married and pool their resources.

My wife and I got married just before our twentieth birthday, and together, we were better able to build our lives. Marriage brought a level of seriousness to my life that called me to be extremely responsible. Studies show that "features of long-term financial stability, such as greater net worth, are positively associated with marriage among young households."[4] Interestingly, "young couples who were living together but not married had median net worth similar to that of young single adults."[5]

When possible, one of the primary purposes of marriage is to bear children and raise them to become godly offspring. In Genesis, God commanded Adam and Eve to be fruitful and multiply, and that mandate has never changed. Children are one of God's greatest gifts (Ps. 127:3-5), and having children helps young men and women mature into adulthood.

God has designed our bodies to respond to parenthood naturally. A young man's brain instantly matures in unique ways once his first child is born. In *The Toxic War on Masculinity*, Nancy Pearcey writes, "In the first few weeks after a child is born, a father's biochemistry changes. His level of testosterone goes down, which makes him less aggressive. At the same time, his level of oxytocin rises, which creates a sense of empathy and bonding. The baby's oxytocin rises as well so that a biochemical bond is forged between the father and his newborn. Their brains begin to function symbiotically. These benefits accrue, however, only if the father is actively holding and playing with his baby."[6] Pearcey summarizes, "In short, becoming a father literally stimulates brain growth."[7]

Studies show that generally, a man's "testosterone production reaches its maximum at about age seventeen, and levels remain high for the next two to three decades,"[8] and a woman's fertility reaches peak levels at age twenty-two.[9] Rather than being the years when young couples start their families, the twenties have become a decade of sensuality, promiscuity, and irresponsibility. We have created a perpetual adolescence that now lasts far into adulthood. In our current unbiblical system, young people are throwing these years away in wild living by participating in sexual activity that God designed for marriage and procreation.

Young women are wasting their most fertile years preparing for and pursuing a career while avoiding one of the highest and most holy callings a woman can experience—becoming a wife and mother. Young men spend these years chasing illicit sexual experiences either in person or virtually. Because of porn addiction and other factors, many young men have stopped pursuing girls and marriage. Many are abandoning God's design entirely by adopting a homosexual lifestyle. Young people have been told that seeking unbridled pleasure is the way to find happiness when, in reality, they are operating outside of God's plan. The result is a society of aimless, unhappy young people.

The number one target of Satan is the family, and the easiest way to destroy a nation is to destroy the nuclear family. The unmarried rate in America has skyrocketed over the last seventy-five years, and many children are being born into homes with unmarried parents and single parents—a recipe for unhealthy, unproductive children. As I mentioned earlier in this book, the rise of fatherlessness has created more societal ills than can be imagined.

God has a beautiful plan for the family, and when we embrace His good design, we create healthy children and societies. Noah saved his children because he fully understood and carried out God's plan for the life of his family. When we reunite with and follow God's plan for our family, He will help us save our children, too.

CHAPTER 25

Noah Won the Hearts and Minds of His Children

*"Parents! It is in your hands to do your children the
greatest kindness, or cruelty, in all the world! Help them
to know God and to be saved, and you do more for them
than if you helped them to be lords or princes."*

Richard Baxter

Somewhere along the line, *Noah won the hearts and minds
of his children.* He became the man they trusted more than
any other on earth. When our girls were growing up, there were
a few times when I thought I was totally failing as a parent.
Nothing tested my parenting skills and challenged my hope
for raising godly offspring like the night our oldest daughter,

Julianna, decided she would not sleep in her bedroom no matter what it cost her. Michele and I had been listening to Dr. Dobson's radio program a lot, and we had purchased his book on the strong-willed child because we had that child. To top it off, she had red hair!

Her now-adult cousins recently told me she would take over whenever she showed up at their house. Even though they were older, she would walk right up to them and yank whatever toy they had out of their hands, and they were too scared to take it back. This challenging persona was really evident until she was about four years old.

In her fourth year, we moved into a new house, and her bedroom was a considerable distance from our bedroom. She instantly decided she did not want to sleep in her new bedroom but wanted to sleep on the floor beside my side of our bed. We allowed this for some time but then heard Dr. Dobson say that you should pick a night and draw a line in the sand. I spent a lot of time and effort explaining to Julianna that she was a big girl and needed to sleep in her own bedroom. She didn't seem too opposed to the idea, so we picked a night and told her she would not be allowed to come into our room unless something unusual happened. I tucked her into her bed in her new room, read her stories, and prayed with her. Everything seemed great, so I went to my room and climbed into bed, relieved that we had finally solved this problem.

Much to my surprise, about fifteen minutes later, I heard something plop down on the floor beside the bed. I rolled over, and low and behold, there she was. I got up and again explained that she had to stay in bed. I took her back to bed, and I even went through the whole bedtime routine again, and all seemed well.

After being in bed for about fifteen minutes, I heard the familiar sound and rolled over, and there she was again. This time, I took her back to bed, applied a little corporal punishment, and got more serious with her about staying in her bed. This started at about 9:30 p.m. and by 4:00 a.m. I was done. I had literally been up all night trying to make her stay in her bed, and my stubborn little girl just kept coming back. I finally gave up and told my wife, "I don't care where she sleeps," and sure enough, she slept right beside me.

When I woke up the next morning, I was sure I had a child headed straight for prison. This little four-year-old girl flat-out whooped her father in that nighttime battle. Trust me, I spanked her. I cajoled her. I tried everything. Nothing fazed her. When I look back on it, I see she was one tough little character. I decided I would give it one more try the following night, knowing that if she kept me up all night again, I would be at a total loss. Amazingly, she never came into my room that second night and slept in her room for the rest of her life. My wife still says Dr. Dobson was wrong and we should have waited a little longer to draw that line in the sand. I tend to believe she's right.

After that experience, Julianna matured and became a wonderful child. She never lost her strong internal fortitude, and today, she is a beautiful wife, a mother to three boys, and an amazing Christian. However, she always asked good questions and never accepted everything I said just because I was her dad. I had to earn her trust and respect. I had to be full of grace and truth in order to win her heart.

Children will not follow a dictator for the long term. They will not follow someone who is all law and no grace. But they love to follow someone who really loves them and whom they love. It is critically important that we win their hearts when they are young so they will allow us to win their minds as they get older.

A TAILORED APPROACH

Our second daughter, Heidi, was a little more pliable, but we still had to earn her trust and love. I discovered she was super tender, and I couldn't be quite as forceful with her because it seemed to crush her. Sure, we disciplined her, but I had to take a little different approach. I remember when Heidi was a teenager, I had given her clear instructions on what to do and what not to do on a certain church teen outing. Early one morning, after getting home from the trip late the night before, she came downstairs, and with a sad voice and tears in her eyes, she told me she had disobeyed me to a fairly minor degree on the trip. I was so pleased with her immediate repentance that I thanked her and did nothing to punish her.

My natural personality leans toward law and order, and I am happy to say I made our girls follow our guidelines. However, more than that, I'm grateful to be able to say that I also poured huge amounts of kindness, love, and tenderness into our girls' lives.

It was a tremendous honor when our daughters told the young men who wanted to date them in college that they would have to meet with their dad first. I had suggested this to my daughters through the years but knew it would ultimately be their decision. Honestly, I was surprised my daughters allowed me to do this, and I'm pretty sure one of them was rolling her eyes when she called me to talk about it. I prepared a questionnaire for these meetings, and thankfully, I now have two wonderful sons-in-law that I love so much.

My girls were old enough to do what they wanted, but they trusted me enough to let me guide them. When it comes to saving our children, it's not all about rules and regulations. We must build a deep and meaningful relationship with them so they will trust us when they need direction and help.

CHAPTER 26

God Wanted Noah to Save His Family

"God's plan and His ways of working out His plan are frequently beyond our ability to fathom and understand. We must learn to trust when we don't understand."

Jerry Bridges

Finally, Noah saved his family because *God wanted Noah to save his family*. At the end of the day, God had to speak to Noah's children and encourage them to get on the ark. As parents, we often grow anxious about whether our children will trust and follow Christ. We recognize our great responsibility and sometimes act as if we can save our children without the help of the Holy Spirit. When they don't respond to our leadership as we hope, we can experience fear and despair.

Even though this section fleshes out how Noah was able to save his family, God is the one who ultimately saved Noah's family. Like Noah, we have a part to play, but we are not the ones who actually save our children. Only Christ can do that.

If you have a child who has gone astray, don't give in to fear and despair. Christ died for your child, and He can reach your child in ways only He understands. Continue to rely on Christ for the salvation of your children, no matter what age or stage they are in life. God gives us the responsibility to do our best and trust Him to do the rest. And He will!

A FAMILY INVENTORY

As we close this section, let's walk through a simple family inventory in order to evaluate our relationships and responsibilities.

1. What is my relationship with Jesus like? Are my spouse, children, and grandchildren seeing me live an authentic Christian life at home? If I'm not walking in a right relationship with Christ, what will I do about it?
2. Do I have a clear picture of God's plan for the family? If not, am I willing to search it out?
3. How is my relationship with my spouse? What am I willing to do to grow in my marriage?
4. Am I willing to stand for truth and be different from the world in how I am raising my children?
5. Am I intentionally training my children at home on what it means to follow Christ?
6. Am I teaching my children and grandchildren about God's truth and equipping them to recognize deception in the world?

7. Am I investing enough time and energy into my children and grandchildren to win their hearts and minds?
8. Am I praying for my children and grandchildren and trusting God to save them?

This inventory may feel overwhelming, especially if you feel you're not doing so well right now. Please don't feel overwhelmed because God wants to help you. You don't have to be perfect, but you have to be honest and willing to change. For biblical worldview resources on parenting, grandparenting, marriage, and growing in your walk with Christ, please visit the resources section at the back of this book. In the closing chapters of this book, we will examine practical steps you can take to help save your children in a world gone crazy.

SECTION 5

Six Practical Steps to
Help You Save Your
Children In a World
Gone Crazy

CHAPTER 27

Acknowledge the Problem With Our Past Approach

"No man or woman ever had a nobler challenge or a higher privilege than to bring up a child for God and whenever we slight that privilege or neglect that ministry for anything else, we live to mourn it in heartache and grief."

Vance Havner

As you approach the end of this book, I pray your heart is filled with a renewed passion to ensure your children and grandchildren know Christ and develop a biblical worldview. Once again, it is important to emphasize that the primary purpose of this book is to ensure you will never have to experience the pain and sadness that comes from your child turning away from God and His teachings and that you will instead witness your children and grandchildren making a positive impact on our world for the glory of God and the good of humanity.

In this closing section, I will summarize six practical steps you can take to help save your children in a world gone crazy. The first step is to *acknowledge that there is a major problem with how we have been raising our children in the evangelical church in America.* As you have seen in the numerous statistics I have provided throughout this book, what we have done for the last fifty years has not worked in helping a majority of children from our Christian homes and churches develop a deep love for Christ, an unshakeable faith, and a biblical worldview. We've all heard the definition of insanity through the years: "Doing the same thing over and over again and expecting a different result." We can't just hope for better results or assume our children will turn out okay.

When less than 5% of American young people hold a biblical worldview, we can conclude that we need to take a new approach to educating and training our children. A lack of deep understanding of God and His plans for the world has affected generations of children thanks to secular education, blended worldviews, superficial church experiences, and insufficient home training. The devil and the world he controls are deeply involved in shaping children's worldviews. Unless we have a greater passion for our children's worldview development than he does, we will inevitably lose them to his awful lies. Every family and church must take on a new sense of urgency, determination, and enthusiasm to save the children in their care.

CHAPTER 28

Evaluate and Manage Your Child's Media Intake

"We must recognize that media is the playground while the heart is the battleground. What happens on a screen is an extension of what is happening in the heart, so help your children guard their hearts and minds and be wise and discerning online."

Dr. Josh Mulvihill

The second practical step you can take to help save your children in a world gone crazy is to *evaluate and manage your child's media intake.* Children today are growing up in a digital world that is unlike any experience in the history of the world. Most of them are connected to devices for the majority of their waking hours, and far too many children are trapped by one or more forms of addiction. Let me give you a real-life example.

I gave a speech to a group of middle and high school students in a Christian school on the four pillars of a biblical worldview. In my second presentation, I talked with them about how to know for sure they were in a genuine relationship with Christ, and as soon as I finished, two sharp young men approached me. They identified themselves as a senior and junior in high school, and I later found out they were two of the best students in the school in every visible way.

The older of the two young men stated in a kind but straightforward manner, "When you gave your first presentation on biblical worldview, I looked at my classmate sitting next to me and said, 'I believe everything he just said, but I don't care.'" Again, he didn't say this disrespectfully or aggressively; he simply stated the facts. I asked him why he didn't care, and he responded by telling me he was so addicted to porn that he was seriously thinking about abandoning Christianity entirely. He told me he was in a small group with other young men trying to conquer this same battle. A man from his church called him daily to hold him accountable, but nothing worked. He was sick and tired of the struggle and just wanted to totally give in to not only porn but many other lusts of the flesh.

I talked with this young man for a long while, and before we parted ways, I prayed over him. In my prayer, I cried out to God and asked Him to reveal His power to this young man. I said, "Lord, this young man must experience You and Your power, or otherwise, I fear he will soon adopt a worldview that will allow him to live in the lust of the flesh." When I finished praying, the young man said, "I can't believe you just prayed like you did." He went on to say, "We were just studying postmodernism in Bible class, and a strong desire sprang up in my heart and said, 'Embrace postmodernism because then you can live any way you want to.'"

GUARDING THEIR HEARTS

Here's the bottom line: We can fill our children with all the truth in the world, but if we do not prevent them from having the desires of their hearts captured by addiction and the lust of the flesh, we will continue to lose them in mass. We must, at all costs, do whatever it takes to prevent our children from being swallowed up by social media, video games, smartphone addiction, porn, and any other form of unhealthy, unbiblical entertainment.

There is a large movement of parents today who are delaying the use of phones, social media, and electronics until later in the teen years because the evidence is overwhelming that these things negatively affect our children and teens. Depression, anxiety, and suicide are astronomically high in the lives of our children today. The chemicals in the brain that are activated with drug use are the same as those involved when children get addicted to screens. We used to say that an ounce of prevention is worth a pound of cure. When it comes to digital addiction, an ounce of prevention is worth a thousand pounds of cure. Once a child is addicted to anything, they lose control of their actions and often spiral into darkness. It's one hundred percent easier to say no *before* a child is addicted than to break the addiction *after* they are caught up in it.

We must lay out our plans regarding media usage for our children in their early childhood and preteen years. Thankfully, some great resources are available to help you know what to do and how to do it. *The Anxious Generation: How the Great*

Rewiring of Childhood Is Causing an Epidemic of Mental Illness by Jonathan Haidt discusses the impact smartphones, social media, and big tech have had on the epidemic of teen mental illness. *Screenstrong.org* provides valuable tips and guides to help kids have fun without screens, develop life skills, and build family relationships. See the resources section at the back of this book for more recommendations for wisely navigating media usage in your home. If we are going to save our children and see them become champions for Christ, we must be willing to take a firm stand on this issue.

CHAPTER 29

Examine Your Child's Educational Experience

"Secularism is the process whereby God and religion are pushed to the margins of life and so make no significant contribution at all to the policies and values adopted by society. By and large, politics and education carry on as if God were not there."

Melvin Tinker

The third practical step you can take to help save your children in a world gone crazy is to *examine their educational experience*. I devoted an entire section of this book to education because this is the one area where the evangelical church and many parents have been slow to understand the role education has played in shaping children's worldviews. Again, a child will spend 16,000 hours at school from kindergarten through twelfth grade. The time they spend at church is minuscule compared to the time they spend at school.

While in school, they are taught by degreed teachers who are seen as the authority on the subject they are teaching and have tremendous influence over how a child understands life and reality. They are also taught from textbooks that seem to hold the ultimate truth about every subject. These textbooks are filled with thousands upon thousands of true and false assumptions that are impossible for a young child to discern and comprehend fully.

Let me just reiterate what I said earlier in this book. Every textbook author has a specific set of beliefs or worldviews from which they write, and every teacher has a specific set of beliefs or worldviews from which they teach. I have often said, "If you give me a child for 16,000 hours, I can make them believe anything I want them to believe." Why do you think the National Education Association is so dead set against all forms of homeschooling or private education? Why do you think Hitler, Stalin, and communist China took over the educational systems immediately after gaining power? They knew that whoever has access to the hearts and minds of the children will determine what they believe and how they live.

American government education is completely hostile to biblical truth. Yes, there are wonderful Christian teachers and administrators who are doing their best to hold back the darkness, but they can only hold back a very small portion of the falsehood and evil that is being taught in non-Christian schools.

I think we can all agree that a child will not develop a biblical worldview as a result of attending any form of secularized education, so if for any reason your child is enrolled in a non-Christian school, you must commit to homeschooling them at night. You can't just ask, "Did you learn anything objectionable today?" They have no idea which of the information they heard was false. You will have to read their textbooks and evaluate what they are required to read online. Ask them lots of questions, and then you must pour truth into them in a very intentional way.

Parents, we only have our children for about eighteen years. I urge you to do everything in your power to make sure you fill their hearts and minds with God's truth and prevent them from being fed lies that could literally ruin their life and even damn their souls for all eternity. This is life and death and nothing less. If you would like to learn more about Christian education options available for your children, please reach out to RenewaNation at info@renewanation.org.

CHAPTER 30

Become a Student of Biblical Worldview

"Here's what we should learn: If we want our children to hear the gospel from us, they must see the gospel's impact upon us. How we live before them powerfully preaches the gospel and its implications for our lives."

Jim Elliff

The fourth practical step you can take to help save your children in a world gone crazy is to *become a student of biblical worldview*. A friend of mine was a family ministry pastor at a very large church. When he first took the position, he was warned to be careful concerning what he said about education to parents because the church didn't want him offending their congregants. After getting his feet down in this new church, he decided he would start training parents and grandparents in biblical worldview so they could better understand the attacks the world was throwing at their children. Many of the parents were clueless about the worldview battle raging for their children's hearts and minds. As my friend trained these parents and grandparents, one family after another made major lifestyle changes, and many re-evaluated how they were training their children at home, how they were connecting their kids to the ministry of the church, and how they were educating their children.

Let me say this with gentleness and kindness: If you are not deeply concerned about what is taught to children in non-Christian schools these days, you need to develop a stronger biblical worldview. A cataclysmic struggle for our children's souls is taking place, and the only way we can lead our children to the truth is to know the truth ourselves. The good news is that many excellent resources are available to us today. A good and simple place to start is by reading the book RenewaNation published by Dr. Josh Mulvihill, titled *Biblical Worldview: What It Is, Why It Matters, and How to Shape the Worldview of the Next Generation*. After this, I encourage you to consider reading books by Francis Schaeffer, Nancy Pearcey, Chuck Colson, and Mama Bear Apologetics. Many more resources to help you develop a biblical worldview are listed at the back of this book.

When you realize Christ is sovereign over all of life and has a beautiful plan for every part of our world, life makes so much sense. Too many Christians live with a Sacred/Secular Divide (SSD) that keeps them from connecting God to all that is happening in their lives and this world. Read good books, watch great videos, and listen to books and podcasts. If you do this, you will be amazed at how much you can help your children and those around you.

In order to be a student of biblical worldview, you will have to lay aside other things that currently dominate your time. You will likely need to watch less television and limit social media. Intentionally schedule times to study and commit to those times. This year, I made a covenant that if I'm not on schedule with my yearly Bible reading plan and my goal of reading one book per week, I will not watch any TV. It has kept me focused, and I'm really enjoying this schedule. We're dealing with eternal destinies, so we must take this seriously!

CHAPTER 31

Fully Commit to a Local Church

"You, as a Christian, were designed and created by God, not for a life of individuality and self-will, but to fill a niche in the spiritual building called the church."

Jim Elliff

The fifth practical step you can take to help save your children in a world gone crazy is to *fully commit to a local church and help that church make a greater impact.* The local church is God-ordained, and every family who wants to raise godly children must be connected to and a committed member of a local body of believers. We cannot raise godly children apart from Christ's body. The Bible doesn't say that a church has to be a specific size or style, but it makes it crystal clear that all Christians who want to grow in their faith and obey the Lord should be deeply connected to a body of believers.

In America, consumerism has taken over the church. Many families move from one church to another during a child's lifetime, and children fail to gain a deep appreciation for life in the body of Christ. Recently, I spoke at a church that had dwindled to only three teens in the teen class and no babies or young children in the church. Rather than packing up and leaving, a group of women gathered and prayed every week for God to fill their church with children. Now, this rural church in the middle of farms is packed with young families who have 170 children and teens. Wherever God calls you to attend church, you must lock in and serve the Lord and the body of believers in that setting.

One of our main goals through our church and family ministry at RenewaNation is to see churches move away from the attractional entertainment model of children and youth ministry and move to a model of equipping parents and grandparents to train children at home. Not long ago, I heard Dr. Josh Mulvihill say that the average evangelical child attends church only 2.5 times per month. We will not make a significant impact if we put all our eggs in the one to two hours a church has children in their care each week. However, if we equip their parents and grandparents with a biblical worldview and give them a vision for training their children at home, our churches can significantly impact the worldview of children.

At RenewaNation, our church and family ministry is a great place to catch a new vision for how your church can give families and children a biblical worldview. Dr. Mulvihill, our Church and Family Ministry Director, has published a book on family ministry in the local church titled *Family Ministry: How Your Church Can Shepherd Parents and Grandparents to Make Disciples*, and Amber Pike, our Family Ministry Coordinator, has published *Intentional Children's Ministry: How Your Church Can Disciple Children With a Lifelong Faith in Jesus*. For these and many other helpful resources, visit church.renewanation. org. These resources will bless you greatly and give you a clear picture of the kind of family ministry that will make your church a powerful tool in helping children become all God wants them to be.

CHAPTER 32

Train Your Children at Home

"Your children should love the Lord, work hard, and experience the joy of trusting God. More important than leaving your children an inheritance is leaving them a spiritual heritage."

Randy Alcorn

The sixth practical step you can take to help save your children in a world gone crazy is to *train them at home.* God has given us, as parents, the responsibility to train our children in God's truth. Yes, we can delegate some of our training to grandparents, friends, pastors, and teachers, but when all is said and done, each parent must personally ensure their children know God and His truth. As parents, we often feel ill-equipped to train our children in the Bible and all the truth it contains. Many parents did not see this modeled when they were growing up. Many Christian families rarely pray together or read and discuss the Bible together. We watch sports and movies together. We go on vacations together and eat meals together, but families rarely sit down and talk about spiritual matters. I'm not exactly sure why this seems so difficult for families, but I know for sure that Satan fights against it.

I highly recommend establishing a rhythm of getting together as a family to pray and discuss the Bible. You will likely have to eat together around your table more to do this. You will have to say no to some other activities. Don't be legalistic, but set reasonable guidelines and boundaries. Maybe you agree no one will turn the TV on or go on social media until the family has taken time to pray together and look into God's Word. It will feel rigid at first, but it will begin to be meaningful after some time.

Beyond spending time training your children in group time, you will need to train each child individually. I mentioned this book earlier, but I am recommending it again because it is one of the most amazing books for intentional training I have ever seen: *50 Things Every Child Needs to Know Before Leaving Home* by Dr. Josh Mulvihill. Josh and I were speaking at a conference in Minnesota one cold Sunday, and he told the most amazing story at the end of one of his speeches that led to the writing of this book.

He told us about the day his parents took him to breakfast when he was seventeen. He said he wasn't sure if he was in trouble or what the special occasion was for him to be able to go out to eat without his siblings in tow. As they sat down, his parents pulled out an old sheet of paper and slid it across the table to him. They then told him that when he was just a little boy, they had sat down and written down everything they wanted him to know before he left home. The list he was holding in his hands was what they had been working on throughout his life, and they asked him to evaluate it and tell them how they had done and what they needed to work on in the last year he would be with them before going to college. Josh didn't even know there was a list, and he was blown away as he looked at it. It was everything from how to study the Bible to small engine repair. He said he told them they had done a pretty good job on most things on the list, but they should give up on small engine repair because there simply wasn't any hope for him in that area.

As Josh was telling this story, my mind was racing with questions. Where was that list his parents used to train Josh and his siblings? His parents raised amazing men and women, so I wanted to see the list they had used! As we went back to the book table at the close of the conference, many young couples came to the table and asked Josh if he had a copy of that list. Unfortunately, Josh didn't have a hard copy, but it was written on his heart and mind. I looked at him that day and said, "That is your next book."

We published the book in the fall of 2021, and it has been a huge blessing to parents across America and beyond. If you want a tremendous guide to help you train your children at home, go to renewanation.org to get your copy today. It's designed to be a keepsake book, one for each child since there's a place to put their picture when they get baptized, cook their first meal, get their driver's license, and much more. There are many other excellent books out there today that will help you train your children at home, and many of these are referenced in this book.

INTENTIONAL GODLY PARENTING AND GRANDPARENTING

Dads and Moms, I encourage you to believe that you can be the greatest influence in the lives of your children. Over the last few years, Michele and I have been privileged to have our first five grandchildren brought into this world. Words can't describe how much we love them. All of you who are grandparents can fully understand.

Our oldest grandson's name is Marshall. He has been privileged to grow up on a 2,000-acre farm and camp. He and I have ridden four-wheelers all over those 2,000 acres. We've gone swimming in the creek with his little brother, Henry, joining us. We've watched cows and goats be born and had about as much fun as you can imagine. Last year, we took Marshall on a week-long vacation with us, and this year, we took Marshall and Henry to Dollywood and Gatlinburg. Cotton candy, ice cream, pancakes, and fun, fun, fun were on the agenda! Yes, we have a ton of fun, but more than that, we are working hard to instill God's love and truth deep in their hearts and minds. Michele and I have fallen in love with our four beautiful grandsons and one granddaughter, and we are fully committed to helping our daughters and sons-in-law raise these children to godly adulthood.

Something significant about our grandchildren dawned on me one day. It is highly likely that Marshall, Henry, Nora, Josiah, and Charlie's children will still be alive one hundred years from right now. Think about it. Marshall is five years old. If he has a child in twenty-five years and that child lives to be seventy-five, that's one hundred years from now. What we are doing with our grandchildren right now will impact the lives of our family long after we have gone to our heavenly home.

For those of you who are currently raising your children,

you are not just affecting the eighteen years you have them in your homes; you are directly impacting the lives of your family for generations to come. This reason is why it's so important that we give our children and grandchildren a biblical worldview. If we do well by our children and grandchildren today, they will do the same for their children and grandchildren. By leading them to Christ and establishing a biblical worldview in their hearts and minds now, we ensure their children and grandchildren will carry forward a long-lasting heritage of faith.

The way we fix what is broken in this world is to regain access to the hearts and minds of our children and grandchildren and pour God's truth into them every single day. As they fall in love with Christ and fully embrace a biblical worldview, God will use them to change our world for His eternal glory.

CHAPTER 33

You Can Do This

"First and foremost, the bringing up of children 'in the nurture and admonition of the Lord' is something that is to be done in the home and by the parents. This is the emphasis throughout the Bible. It is not something that is to be handed over to the school, however good the school may be. It is the duty of parents—their primary and most essential duty."

Dr. Martin Lloyd Jones

Perhaps you are one of the millions of parents in America who have had a total awakening since 2020. You now fully understand the battle that is raging for the hearts and minds of your children, and you are up for the fight. I want to honor and commend you. God is using you and millions of others just like you to raise up a new generation of Christian thinkers and leaders whom He will use to bring great hope to our lost world.

Maybe you're a parent who hasn't yet joined this great parental awakening, but after reading the message in this book, there is a fire burning in your heart to join this new movement. I must warn you that the devil will do everything in his power to stop you. He hates seeing children taught the truth and knows he is no match for godly, Spirit-filled parents on a mission to save their children. The devil will use friends and family members to work against your new commitment to ensure your children develop a biblical worldview.

Many who have not yet been awakened will not understand the changes you will make in how you are raising your children and who you are allowing to have influence in their lives. When you make changes in the areas of education, family, church, and how you allow your children to interact with culture, most will not immediately understand or agree with you. That's okay. Be patient with them. Remember, not long ago, you didn't understand the necessity of some of the changes you are now making. Pray for those who oppose you, and place this book and other books like it in their hands when possible. Don't be preachy or judgmental. Practice love and kindness, and let the Holy Spirit do the work only He can do in their hearts.

COMMIT TO KNOW, LOVE, AND SERVE JESUS

Every time I get home from a ministry trip, I go by and sit down with my elderly parents. My father preached in thirty-eight nations, and he and my mom gave everything they had to raise godly children and serve Christ's kingdom. Dad isn't able to travel or preach much these days, and Mom often doesn't have the strength to make it to church. Each time I stop by, they want a report on my trip and how God worked in the lives of those I spoke to or met with. As I get up to leave, they always tell me how proud they are of me and of the fact that I'm giving my whole life to Christ and His grand purposes on earth. Occasionally, Dad will express regret that he can't go out and preach like he used to. He's even shared with me that sometimes he struggles with the temptation to believe that maybe his ministry is over. I'm always so glad to tell my father, "Your ministry isn't over. It's only just beginning!" I remind him that, as of the writing of this book, ninety-two of his direct descendants serve in Christian vocational ministry. Because my mom and dad loved Jesus with all their hearts and made serving Him the number one goal for all our lives, they are reaping the reward of their commitment in their closing years.

Imagine with me for a moment where you and your children will be in one hundred years. All who are alive now will then likely be in eternity. I can think of nothing greater than spending all of eternity with my children and grandchildren in the safety, security, and beauty of heaven and our Savior, the Lord Jesus Christ. If you love going on a vacation with your family, then you will love heaven! It will be the most glorious, never-ending vacation one could ever imagine. All difficulties and fears will be gone forever, and we will experience the fulfillment of every longing in our hearts for happiness and joy. In the meantime, if we lead our children to Christ and help them develop a biblical worldview, we will have the joy of watching them become passionate followers of Christ and make a significant difference in this world.

Dads and Moms, this is your day! With God's help, you can do this!

A SPECIAL MESSAGE

Dear Friends,

Thank you so much for taking the time to read this book, which has so many important things to say to parents and grandparents. If you would like to let us know how this book impacted you, please email your thoughts to cfam@renewanation.org.

If you agree that every parent should read this book, join us in our efforts to get this book into the hands of thousands of more parents. Please consider taking the following action:

1. Go to shop.renewanation.org and purchase additional copies to give to each person in your family who is currently raising children. To purchase more than 10 copies, call RenewaNation at 540-890-8900 or email info@renewanation.org for a 30% discount on each book.

2. Consider going to renewanation.org/cfam to offer a gift of any amount so RenewaNation can continue to print and distribute these books to families across America.

Thank you so much for your partnership with The Collingsworth Family and RenewaNation in this great effort.

Phil & Kim Collingsworth

FEEDBACK

If God has used this book to help you in any way, please share your story with us at info@renewanation.org, Jeff's Facebook page (Jeff Keaton), or X account (@jeffkeaton1). We would be honored to know how God is using this book to impact your life.

If you would like to give this book to others, please contact RenewaNation at info@renewanation.org to receive a bulk rate price for ten or more books.

Would you like to learn more about bringing Jeff Keaton to your community?

Jeff speaks to groups of parents, grandparents, pastors, and educators all across America and beyond. If you appreciate this book, you will be blessed by his ability to communicate this message clearly and passionately in person. Call RenewaNation at 540-890-8900 or email info@renewanation.org to begin the discussion.

ENDNOTES

CHAPTER 1:
1. "CA Law Would Help Children Get Gender Transition Surgery Without Parental Consent," Family Freedom Project, Accessed October 9, 2024, https://www.familyfreedomproject.org/ca-law-would-help-children-get-gender-transition-surgery.
2. George Barna, *Raising Spiritual Champions: Nurturing your Child's Heart, Mind, and Soul* (Arizona Christian University Press, 2023), 22.

CHAPTER 2:
1. Henry W.F. Saggs, "Babylon," Encyclopedia Britannica, August 18, 2024, https://www.britannica.com/place/Babylon-ancient-city-Mesopotamia-Asia.
2. Jack Zavada, "Biblical History of Ancient Babylon," Learn Religions, December 4, 2019, https://www.learnreligions.com/history-of-babylon-3867031.
3. Ibid.
4. Matthew George Easton, Easton's Bible Dictionary (Harper & Brothers, 1893), as found in the Logos Bible Software program.
5. Edited by J. D. Barry, The Lexham Bible Dictionary (Bellingham, WA: Lexham Press, 2016), as found in the Logos Bible Software program.
6. "Shadrach, Meshach, Abednego," Bible Gateway, Accessed April 23, 2024, https://www.biblegateway.com/resources/encyclopedia-of-the-bible/Shadrach-Meshach-Abednego.
7. "What's In A Name," Institute for Creation Research, Accessed April 23, 2024, https://www.icr.org/article/whats-name.
8. "Meshach," Behind the Name, Accessed April 23, 2024, https://www.behindthename.com/name/shadrach.
9. Edited by J. D. Barry, The Lexham Bible Dictionary (Bellingham, WA: Lexham Press, 2016), as found in the Logos Bible Software program.
10. "Why did Nebuchadnezzar change Daniel's name to Belteshazzar?" Got Questions Ministries, Accessed April 23, 2024, https://www.gotquestions.org/Daniel-Belteshazzar.html.

CHAPTER 3:
1. "Back-to-school statistics," National Center for Education Statistics, Accessed October 17, 2024, https://www.nces.ed.gov/fastfacts/display.asp?id=372.

CHAPTER 4:
1. Jack Kelly, "The Rise In DINKs, SINKs, DINKWADs, KIPPERs And More," Forbes, June 21, 2024, https://www.forbes.com/sites/jackkelly/2024/06/20/the-rise-in-dinks-sinks-dinkwads-kippers.

2. Anna Fleck, "Americans Are Getting Married Older Than Ever," Statista, December 15, 2023, https://www.statista.com/chart/7031/americans-are-tying-the-knot-older-than-ever.

3. Emily Sherman, "DINKs Report Less Stress, More Savings in 2024: MarketWatch Guides Survey," MarketWatch Guides, September 24, 2024, https://www.marketwatch.com/guides/savings/dinks-survey-2024.

4. "The Lancet: Dramatic declines in global fertility rates set to transform global population patterns by 2100" Institute For Health Metrics and Evaluation, March 20, 2024, https://www.healthdata.org/news-events/newsroom/news-releases/lancet-dramatic-declines-global-fertility-rates-set-transform.

5. Jennifer Calfas and Anthony DeBarros, "U.S. Fertility Rate Falls to Record Low," The Wall Street Journal, Accessed October 18, 2024, https://www.msn.com/en-us/health/other/u-s-fertility-rate-falls-to-record-low/ar-AA1nCnTn.

6. Servet Yanatma, "Europe's fertility crisis: Which countries are having the most and fewest babies?," Euronews, September 28, 2024, https://www.euronews.com/health/2024/09/28/europes-fertility-crisis-which-european-country-is-having-the-fewest-babies.

7. "Europe's Growing Muslim Population," Pew Research Center, November 29, 2017, https://www.pewresearch.org/religion/2017/11/29/europes-growing-muslim-population.

8. Ibid.

9. Michael Lipka and Conrad Hackett, "Why Muslims are the world's fastest-growing religious group," Pew Research Center, April 6, 2017, https://www.pewresearch.org/short-reads/2017/04/06/why-muslims-are-the-worlds-fastest-growing-religious-group.

10. "The Lancet: Dramatic declines in global fertility rates set to transform global population patterns by 2100" Institute For Health Metrics and Evaluation, March 20, 2024, https://www.healthdata.org/news-events/newsroom/news-releases/lancet-dramatic-declines-global-fertility-rates-set-transform.

11. Ibid.

12. Yaqiu Wang, "It's time to abolish China's three-child policy," Global Institute for Women's Leadership, Kings College London, February 22, 2023, https://www.hrw.org/news/2023/02/22/its-time-abolish-chinas-three-child-policy.

13. "Female infanticide in China," Wikipedia, Accessed October 18, 2024, https://www.en.m.wikipedia.org/wiki/Female_infanticide_in_China.

14. Ibid.

15. Ibid.

16. Bridge Education Services, "Christian School Education in China," ChinaSource, April 9, 2024, https://www.chinasource.org/resource-library/blog-entries/christian-school-education-in-china.

17. "Measuring Religion in China" Pew Research Center, August 30, 2023, https://www.pewresearch.org/religion/2023/08/30/measuring-religion-in-china.

CHAPTER 5:

1. "Six Reasons Young Christians Leave Church," Barna Group, September 27, 2011, https://www.barna.com/research/six-reasons-young-christians-leave-church.

2. Michael Catt (@MichaelCatt), "Whoever wants the next generation the most will get them," X, September 10, 2020, 7:12 AM, https://www.x.com/MichaelCatt/status/1304014957521121281.

CHAPTER 7:

1. George Barna, *Raising Spiritual Champions: Nurturing your Child's Heart, Mind, and Soul* (Arizona Christian University Press, 2023), 23.

CHAPTER 9:

1. Dr. Tracy F. Munsil, "Biblical Worldview Among U.S. Adults Drops 33% Since Start of COVID-19 Pandemic," Barna Group, February 28, 2023, https://www.arizonachristian.edu/2023/02/28/biblical-worldview-among-u-s-adults-drops-33-since-start-of-covid-19-pandemic.

CHAPTER 10:

1. CRC Staff, "Most US Kids Ages 8-12 Lack Biblical 'Cornerstones,' Research Says," Barna Group, October 11, 2023, https://www.arizonachristian.edu/2023/10/11/most-us-kids-ages-8-12-lack-biblical-cornerstones.
2. Ibid.
3. Ibid.
4. Ibid.
5. Dr. Christian Overman, "SSD: A Virus with Devastating Consequences for America," RenewaNation, Accessed October 25, 2024, https://www.renewanation.org/post/ssd-a-virus-with-devastating-consequences-for-america.

CHAPTER 11:

1. Bill Muehlenberg, "Machen, Education and the State," CultureWatch, August 5, 2018, https://billmuehlenberg.com/2018/08/05/machen-education-and-the-state.
2. "Of Education," The John Milton Reading Room, Accessed October 25, 2024, https://milton.host.dartmouth.edu/reading_room/of_education/text.shtml.

CHAPTER 13:

1. George Barna, *Raising Spiritual Champions: Nurturing your Child's Heart, Mind, and Soul* (Arizona Christian University Press, 2023), 22.
2. Ibid., 23-24.
3. Ibid., 23.
4. Nancy Pearcey (@NancyRPearcey), "Scientists cannot live out the materialist worldview they profess…," X, May 12, 2024, 3:28 PM, https://x.com/NancyRPearcey/status/1789739553089065440.
5. Nancy R. Pearcey and Charles B. Thaxton, *The Soul of Science: Christian Faith and Natural Philosophy* (Crossway Books, 1994), 19.

CHAPTER 14:

1. Russell Howard Tuttle, "human evolution," Encyclopaedia Britannica, October 21, 2024, https://www.britannica.com/science/human-evolution.
2. "New Analysis Shows U.S. Imposes Long Prison Sentences More Frequently than Other Nations," The Council on Criminal Justice, December 20, 2022, https://counciloncj.org/new-analysis-shows-u-s-imposes-long-prison-sentences-more-frequently-than-other-nations.

CHAPTER 15:

1. "Of Education," The John Milton Reading Room, Accessed October 25, 2024, https://milton.host.dartmouth.edu/reading_room/of_education/text.shtml.

2. R. Austin McCormick, "Expect Great Things, Attempt Great Things," Covenant Baptist Theological Seminary, June 9, 2022, https://cbtseminary. org/expect-great-things-attempt-great-things-r-austin-mccormick.

CHAPTER 16:
1. Hillary Morgan Ferrer and Amy Davison, *Mama Bear Apologetics Guide to Sexuality: Empowering Your Kids to Understand and Live Out God's Design* (Harvest House Publishers, 2021).
2. Ibid.
3. Ibid.
4. Allie Beth Stuckey (@conservmillen), "Because 'science' is an insufficient guide…," X, June 4, 2024, 10:40 PM, https://x. com/conservmillen/status/1798183050733334745.

CHAPTER 17:
1. Jane Anderson, "The impact of family structure on the health of children: Effects of divorce," National Library of Medicine, Accessed October 25, 2024, https://pmc.ncbi.nlm.nih.gov/articles/PMC4240051.
2. "The Extent of Fatherlessness," fathers.com, Accessed October 25, 2024, https://fathers.com/the-extent-of-fatherlessness.
3. "Research and Statistics," Rochester Area Fatherhood Network, Accessed October 25, 2024, https://www.rochesterareafatherhoodnetwork.org/statistics.
4. Anna Sutherland, "Yes, Father Absence Causes the Problems It's Associated With," The Institute for Family Studies, February 4, 2014, https://ifstudies. org/blog/yes-father-absence-causes-the-problems-its-associated-with.
5. "Research and Statistics," Rochester Area Fatherhood Network, Accessed October 25, 2024, https://www.rochesterareafatherhoodnetwork.org/statistics.
6. Rob Wood (@coachrobwood), "Statistics on fatherlessness…," X, March 12, 2024, 3:11 PM, https://x.com/coachrobwood/status/1767629455193715126.

CHAPTER 19:
1. "An Overview of Healthy Childhood Sexual Development," The National Children's Advocacy Center, https://www.nationalcac.org/ wp-content/uploads/2016/08/HealthySexualDevelopmentOverview.pdf.

CHAPTER 20:
1. D. James Kennedy, *What If Jesus Had Never Been Born?* (Thomas Nelson, 2008).

CHAPTER 24:
1. The Feminist Turned HouseWife (@antifemwife), "In 1910 almost…," X, September 3, 2024, 12:08 PM, https://x. com/antifemwife/status/1831001416980214242.
2. Scott Stanley and Galena Rhoades, "What's the Plan? Cohabitation, Engagement, and Divorce," Institute for Family Studies, Accessed October 25, 2024, https://ifstudies.org/reports/ whats-the-plan-cohabitation/2023/executive-summary.
3. Jesse Smith and Nicholas H. Wolfinger, "Testing Common Theories on the Relationship Between Premarital Sex and Marital Stability," Institute for Family Studies, March 6, 2023,

https://ifstudies.org/blog/testing-common-theories-on-the-relationship-between-premarital-sex-and-marital-stability.

4. Fenaba R. Addo and Lowell R. Ricketts, "As Fewer Young Adults Wed, Married Couples' Wealth Surpasses Others," The Federal Reserve Bank of St. Louis, January 1, 2019, https://www.stlouisfed.org/publications/in-the-balance/2018/as-fewer-young-adults-wed.

5. Ibid.

6. Nancy Pearcey (@NancyRPearcey), "Fathers get a biochemical boost…," X, November 9, 2023, 4:03 PM, https://x.com/NancyRPearcey/status/1722721551190040999.

7. Ibid.

8. "Testosterone, aging, and the mind," Harvard Health Publishing, January 1, 2008, https://www.health.harvard.edu/newsletter_article/testosterone_aging_and_the_mind.

9. Robin E. Jensen, Nicole Martins, and Melissa M. Parks, "Public Perception of Female Fertility: Initial Fertility, Peak Fertility, and Age-Related Infertility Among U.S. Adults," National Library of Medicine, Accessed October 25, 2024, https://pubmed.ncbi.nlm.nih.gov/29582267.

RESOURCES

RESOURCES FOR ADULTS AND TEENS:

Some of these resources contain mature themes.
Parental discretion is advised.

Biblical Worldview:

Answers Volumes 1-4 by Answers in Genesis

Biblical Worldview: What It Is, Why It Matters, and How to Shape the Worldview of the Next Generation by Dr. Josh Mulvihill

Cold-Case Christianity: A Homicide Detective Investigates the Claims of the Gospels by J. Warner Wallace

Evidence That Demands a Verdict: Life-Changing Truth for a Skeptical World by Josh McDowell and Sean McDowell

Five Lies of Our Anti-Christian Age by Rosaria Butterfield

How Now Shall We Live? by Charles Colson and Nancy Pearcey

How Should We Then Live?: The Rise and Decline of Western Thought and Culture by Francis A. Schaeffer

Marriage and the Family: Biblical Essentials by Andreas J. Kostenberger and David W. Jones

One Race One Blood: The Biblical Answer to Racism by Ken Ham and Charles Ware

The New Answers Books from Answers in Genesis

The RenewaNation Review Magazine from RenewaNation

Thinking Biblically: Recovering a Christian Worldview by John MacArthur

Total Truth: Liberating Christianity from Its Cultural Captivity by Nancy Pearcey

True Woman 101: Divine Design: An Eight-Week Study on Biblical Womanhood by Mary A. Kassian and Nancy Leigh DeMoss

Who Am I? Solving the Identity Puzzle by Martin Iles

Why Social Justice Is Not Biblical Justice: An Urgent Appeal to Fellow Christians in a Time of Social Crisis by Scott David Allen

Family Ministry and the Local Church:

Family Ministry: How Your Church Can Shepherd Parents and Grandparents to Make Disciples by Dr. Josh Mulvihill

Intentional Children's Ministry: How Your Church Can Disciple Children with a Lifelong Faith in Jesus by Amber Pike

Grandparenting:

Biblical Grandparenting by Dr. Josh Mulvihill

Discipling Your Grandchildren by Dr. Josh Mulvihill with Jen Mulvihill and Linda Weddle

Grandparenting with a Purpose: Effective Ways to Pray for Your Grandchildren by Lillian Ann Penner

Long-Distance Grandparenting by Wayne Rice

Prayers that Stir the Hearts of Grandparents by Sherry Schumann

Raising Your Grandchildren by Cavin Harper

Marriage:

Loving Your Wife as Christ Loved the Church by Larry E. McCall

Strengthening Your Marriage by Wayne A. Mack

The Excellent Wife: A Biblical Perspective by Martha Peace

Media:

12 Ways Your Phone Is Changing You by Tony Reinke

Screenstrong.org

The Anxious Generation: How the Great Rewiring of Childhood Is Causing an Epidemic of Mental Illness by Jonathan Haidt

The Tech-Wise Family: Everyday Steps for Putting Technology in its Proper Place by Andy Crouch

Parenting:

50 Things Every Child Needs to Know Before Leaving Home by Dr. Josh Mulvihill

*Family Shepherds: Calling and Equipping Men to
Lead Their Homes* by Voddie Baucham Jr.

*Mama Bear Apologetics Guide to Sexuality: Empowering
Your Kids to Understand and Live Out God's Design*
by Hillary Morgan Ferrer and Amy Davison

*Preparing Children for Marriage: How to Teach Children God's Good
Design for Marriage, Sex, Dating, and Purity* by Dr. Josh Mulvihill

*Raising Spiritual Champions: Nurturing Your Child's
Heart, Mind, and Soul* by Dr. George Barna

Shepherding a Child's Heart by Tedd Tripp

*The War on Children: Providing Refuge for Your
Children in a Hostile World* by John MacArthur

Podcasts:

Biblical Worldview Show with Ben Schettler

Breakpoint with John Stonestreet

Parenting with Ginger Hubbard

The Briefing with Albert Mohler

The Christian Worldview with David Wheaton

Spiritual Growth:

Bitesize Theology: An ABC of the Christian Faith by Peter Jeffery

Discipleship Course for New Christians by Jeff Keaton (If you
have trusted Christ for salvation as a result of reading this
book, please contact us at info@renewanation.org to receive
this resource to help you in your new walk with Christ.)

Foundational Truths: A Modern Catechism by Israel Wayne

*The Epic Story of the Bible: How to Read and
Understand God's Word* by Greg Gilbert

RESOURCES FOR CHILDREN AND TEENS:

Biblical Foundation:

Big Theology For Little Hearts Series by Devon Provencher (Babies and Preschoolers)

Big Truths for Little Hearts: Theology Cards for Kids from The Daily Grace Co. (Babies and Preschoolers)

Drive Thru History with Dave Stotts (Elementary Age/Middle School)

Foundational Truths: A Modern Catechism by Israel Wayne (Elementary Age)

Seeds Kids Worship (Elementary Age)

The 10 Minute Bible Journey by Dale Mason (Elementary Age/Middle School/Teens)

Biblical Worldview:

Answers Book for Teens from Answers in Genesis (Middle School)

Answers Magazine from Answers in Genesis (Middle School/Teens)

Biblical Worldview Show with Ben Schettler (Middle School/Teens)

Case for Christ for Kids by Lee Strobel (Elementary Age)

God Made Boys and Girls: Helping Children Understand the Gift of Gender by Marty Machowski (Preschool/Elementary)

Kids Answers Magazine from Answers in Genesis (Elementary Age)

One Blood for Kids: What the Bible Says about Race by Ken Ham (Elementary Age)

Science Confirms the Bible (DVD) by Ken Ham (Middle School/Teens)

The Answers Books for Kids from Answers in Genesis (Elementary Age)

The Case for Christ by Lee Strobel (Middle School/Teens)

The Moon Is Always Round by Jonathan Gibson (Preschool/Elementary Age)

What Does The Bible Say About That?: A Biblical Worldview Curriculum For Children by Kevin Swanson (Elementary Age/Middle School)

This is an abbreviated list of resources, and many other excellent resources are available for developing a biblical worldview.

Transforming culture by giving millions of children a biblical worldview

RenewaNation

Our mission is to inspire and equip the family, church, and school to give the children in their care a biblical worldview.

Main Website: **renewanation.org**

Christian Education Division: **reap.renewanation.org**

Church and Family Division: **church.renewanation.org**

Manderley Christian Camp: **manderley.camp**

Manderley Farms: **manderleyfarms.com**

renewanation.org | **540-890-8900**

Raising Children to Godly Adults

PUT A BIBLICAL PLAN INTO ACTION TO RAISE CHILDREN TO MATURITY IN CHRIST

50 Things Every Child Needs to Know Before Leaving Home is a guidebook to help parents chart a course to holistically disciple their child to mature, godly adulthood while also functioning as a keepsake that will allow parents to capture milestones and memories associated with each of the fifty areas to give to a child when he or she is older. It's designed to help you establish a plan and be proactive for each season of your parenting journey in the following areas of your child's life:

- Firm foundations
- Christlike character development
- Biblical beliefs and worldview
- Spiritual growth
- Life skills
- Relational skills
- Work and money management
- Home management
- Personal care
- Educational essentials

"This book is a game changer. A must have in equipping parents to raise children with lifelong faith in Christ. Highly recommend it!"

Pat Williams - NBA Hall of Famer and Author of over 120 Books

shop.renewanation.org

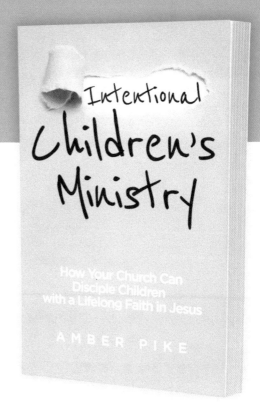

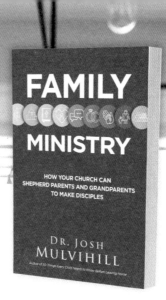

CAPTURE A BIBLICAL VISION FOR FAMILY MINISTRY

Family Ministry will help your church shepherd parents and grandparents to make disciples. Discover what family ministry is, why it matters, and how to establish a family ministry in your church as we explore nine biblical characteristics of a vibrant family ministry. It's a helpful resource for senior pastors, executive pastors, men's and women's ministry leaders, children's pastors, youth pastors—anyone that cares about family discipleship.

SHOP.RENEWANATION.ORG

The
Biblical
Worldview
Show

A MINISTRY OF RENEWANATION

PODCAST

Join host Ben Schettler and expert authors and speakers as we look to the Word of God for answers to the tough questions culture is asking. Find truth in the midst of lies, clarity in the chaos, and practical help for the road ahead on The Biblical Worldview Show.

LISTEN NOW

biblicalworldviewshow.com